Quintet: Five One-Act Plays

Sarah Walton Miller

Broadman Press
Nashville, Tennessee

© Copyright 1981 • Broadman Press
All rights reserved
4275-20
ISBN Number: 0-8054-7520-6

Dewey Decimal Classification: 812
Subject Heading: DRAMA—COLLECTIONS
Library of Congress Catalog Card Number: 80-69242

Printed in the United States of America

CONTENTS

FOREWORD

The one-act plays in this book are suitable for presentation in the church auditorium or other locations in the church. Staging is simple. The lighting suggested in two of them need not require elaborate equipment. A little ingenuity will find a way. Even a slide projector can be a spotlight.

The plays can be performed by young people or adults. Why not age-cast plays, using all suitable ages?

"Brief Rebellion" is a modern play which shows what could happen in a family growing apart rather than together.

"Veil to Treason" is the result of research into the puzzle of Judas. Many scholars believe him to have been totally misguided. That does not make him any less a traitor, but it does make him more understandable.

"The Barrier" is the author's imagination dealing with what happened to Mary Magdalene after the resurrection. The Bible gives no clues. Lest some purists be offended at the humanness of hitherto sacred characters, please remember they *were* human, not perfect, not above the failures of all humanity.

Two of the plays are meant for fellowship occasions such as banquets or parties. "Case for Samaria" is entirely imaginary, based on the story of the Good Samaritan, looking in on the characters twenty years later. The other play is "Love Triumphant" or "Sheriff, Arrest That Man!" It is an old-fashioned melodrama, intended to be dramatically over-acted.

SARAH WALTON MILLER

BRIEF REBELLION

SCENE: The living room of the Bradshaw home. There should be two exits: one to the interior and one to exterior. If the play is staged in a church sanctuary, use folding chairs for a sofa and other seating. Place the phone and papers on any table that is available.

TIME: Early Saturday afternoon

CAST: Dick Bradshaw, *fifteen;* Betty Johnson, *the girl next door;* Martha, *Dick's mother;* Tom, *his father;* Henry and Agnes Alcott, *friends and fellow church members. Agnes is a scatterbrained woman who speaks in capitals.*

(As the play begins, Betty enters from exterior and calls out.)

BETTY: Dick? Dick!
DICK *(from interior):* Coming! *(Enters.)* Hi, Betty.
BETTY: Are you using your tennis rackets today?
DICK: Neither one. Want them?
BETTY: Just one. Jerry has his. We thought we'd play on those clay courts awhile.

DICK: I'll get it. *(Goes interior.)*
BETTY *(calling to him):* Want to go? We could get Ann.

DICK *(from interior):* I'm going fishing.

BETTY *(surprised):* You're *what?*

DICK *(returning with racket):* I'm going fishing. With *Dad.* *(Betty looks doubtful.)* Well, he promised! Maybe he really will go. This time.

BETTY *(sits):* I hope so.

DICK *(sits beside her, glumly):* Yeah.

BETTY: Does he know it's not just the fishing? Have you told him?

DICK: I tried a couple of times. He doesn't hear me.

BETTY: Don't set your heart on it, Dick.

DICK *(bursting out):* He *has* to keep his word this time! I've just about had it!

BETTY *(puts her hand over his):* Don't.

DICK: Why not?

BETTY: Is your mother here?

DICK: Upstairs. Temporarily.

BETTY: Temporarily?

DICK: Wouldn't you know there was something at the church this morning? She came back a few minutes ago. She's dressing now for something else. At the church.

BETTY: Again?

DICK *(bitterly):* Don't you know nothing ever goes on at that church without her or Dad there? Or both of them.

BETTY: Now, Dick . . .

DICK *(jumps up):* It's the truth! I think they're scared someone else will get to run something if they don't watch out!

BETTY *(rising):* Well—if you need me for anything, yell out the window. Until Jerry comes, anyway. I'll keep my fingers crossed. Thanks for the racket.

DICK: Okay. Tell old Jer, hi!

(Betty leaves. Dick goes interior, brings fishing gear. Sits, looking over lures and flies. A bright red one in his hand. Martha enters from interior, a purse in her hand.)

6

MARTHA: Was that Betty? Did you fix yourself a sandwich? *(She doesn't wait for an answer.)* Oh, dear, I know I'm forgetting something! *(sees tackle)* Oh! You and Tom are going fishing!

DICK: He promised, anyway.

MARTHA *(absently):* My notebook! Now, where did I put that notebook? *(Looks through papers beside phone. Phone rings)* Hello ... Mr. Bradshaw isn't here. This is Mrs. Bradshaw. No, I can't tell you where to reach him. What was that number again? *(Writes on pad.)* I have it. Yes, I'll tell him. Good-bye.

DICK *(morosely):* It's after two. He's broken so many promises.

MARTHA: When he breaks a promise, there's a good reason.

DICK: A promise ought to be a promise!

MARTHA: Don't be childish, Dick. Your father is a busy man. *(Begins looking in her purse.)*

DICK: Yeah. We meet at breakfast, sometime. We ride to church in the same car, sometime. He's never home. Either of you! With Dad it's his business or the church business. He runs every committee there whether he's on it or not!

MARTHA: Don't be a baby. Have your Dad call that number. It's important, Dick.

DICK *(sarcastically):* Church business?

MARTHA *(complacently):* Yes, as it happens. They call him about everything. I don't know what they'd do at that church without your father.

DICK: If he dropped dead they'd have to call someone else.

MARTHA *(annoyed):* Now, Dick! A fifteen-year-old boy pouting like a child! It's time you grew up. *(Phone rings.)* Hello.

DICK *(sarcastically):* I can't remember an evening we all spent together in months. And I think I would remember!

MARTHA *(into phone):* Yes, I won't forget. Tuesday at eight. Thank you for reminding me. Good-bye. *(To Dick.)* Another meeting. So many things to do. Where *is* that notebook? Oh, and that swatch of materials! *(She exits interior.)*

DICK *(calling after her): We* need something, too, Mom. A family needs time together!

MARTHA *(from inside):* Later, Dick!

DICK *(goes toward exit and shouts):* Somebody else would do some of these things if you'd let them, I'll bet! Why don't you, Mom? What's the real reason?

MARTHA *(from inside):* Now, Dick! Everything we do is for you, too.
DICK: Don't I have any choice?
MARTHA *(re-enters, notebook and swatch in hand):* Dick, what is the matter with you? We do what is best for you because we care about you.

DICK *(slumps on chair):* Do you? How can you tell? Know what I think? I think you love managing that church and being the big shots more than anything in the world!

MARTHA *(coldly):* What a ridiculous thing to say! Your father and I should not have to explain our motives for doing the Lord's work. We do what we do because we love the Lord. And because we have more experience than others. Not for—well, whatever you might think.

DICK: You wouldn't admit it.
MARTHA: Let's drop the subject! I don't know why you are so worked up, anyway. *(Opens notebook.)* Better jot down that Tuesday date. *(Does so. Now speaks lightly.)* I couldn't go to any meeting without this. Today we are choosing colors and fabrics for the new nursery. It is a good committee except for Minnie Simpson. She has such a mind of her own about what the *children* want. When visitors come to inspect our facilities I want them to be impressed by the good taste evident. I can handle Minnie! *(Notices Dick fingering bright red lure. Makes effort to be interested.)* Dick, I'm sure Tom will go this time. Is that a new lure?

8

DICK: Yes.

MARTHA *(making conversation)*: Something special?

DICK *(responding in spite of himself. Brings it to her)*: Yes. I thought I'd let Dad break it in on that rod Uncle Christopher sent me.

MARTHA: Well, have a good time. Tell your father to take a sweater. It gets chilly and he catches cold so easily. I must rush. It would never do for me to be late! *(Exits exterior.)*

(Dick puts lure in pocket, gets the sweater for his father and is re-checking gear when phone rings.)

DICK: Hello. No, he isn't. I will. 503-8211. Okay. *(Adds number to pad. Wanders back to gear. Tom enters from exterior, preoccupied. Begins to go through papers beside the phone.)*

TOM: Dick, did you see those specifications I brought home the other night? About chairs and table. From Smith and Sons, and the Brackett Company. A yellow sheet and a white, stapled together.

DICK: No.

TOM: I'm sure I—are these numbers for me to call? *(Dick nods. Tom dials.)* Tom Bradshaw here. Yes. Well, I told them that material was no good for our purpose. I don't care what Higgins said, that material is no good! Use the stuff you showed me. Of course it's all right. Don't worry about the committee. I'll handle them. That all? Okay, good-bye. *(Dials again.)* Tom Bradshaw. No, he didn't say anything to me about it. Well, it'll have to have my okay. All right, all right, call a meeting, if you must! Yes, yes, I know. Not Monday, I'm tied up. Say, Thursday night at nine. I know that's late but it's then or late in the next week. Okay, okay. You set it up. Goodbye. *(Hangs up, starts interior, sees gear.)* Oh! We were going fishing this afternoon, weren't we?

DICK: At two. It's past two-thirty now.

TOM: I'm sorry. We'll have to postpone it.

DICK: Again?

9

TOM: Something came up about the furniture for the new educational wing.

DICK: After you promised?

TOM: Company representatives are meeting me at three.

DICK: Did *they* ask you for the meeting?

TOM: Now, Dick—

DICK: Can't you meet Monday?

TOM: Too late.

DICK: Then how about someone else meeting with them?

TOM: No one knows the setup like I do.

DICK *(sarcastically):* You could *tell* them. There are a couple other intelligent men around that church besides you!

TOM: Cut out the sarcasm!

DICK: You want that meeting! It means that much to you, doesn't it?

TOM *(provoked):* The deal's got to be settled today my way or two of the deacons will bring up an alternate proposal Monday!

DICK: Of course *your* way's best?

TOM: What *is* all this?

DICK: Couldn't someone else's way be just as good?

TOM: I've spent a lot of time on this decision!

DICK: I'll bet! Too bad *I'm* not chairs and tables!

TOM *(irritated):* Now, Dick, it's juvenile remarks like that—well, some things come before pleasure. This is the Lord's work.

DICK *(sharply):* Is it?

TOM *(holding his temper forcibly):* Richard! The Lord's work takes first place over personal affairs.

DICK You have a special summons from on high to do it all by yourself? Tom Bradshaw, big wheel! *(Turns his back on his father.)*

TOM *(sarcastically):* You might recall that a large number of members feel they have done their Christian duty if they attend services occasionally. Someone has to *see* after things.

DICK*(turning):* And you are the *chosen?* Dad, you don't own that church and you aren't the only one in it. It isn't fair to others for you to have so much say. Besides every family needs to spend time together. The fellows I know go fishing with their Dads. They *talk*. It isn't a sin, you know! What's more, the walls of their churches are all standing!

TOM: What do you want me to do? Give up all my work at the church? Is that it? *(Dick just looks and doesn't answer.)* Well, answer me! Is that it?

DICK *(slowly):* You have the company. You are top dog there. Why not ease off a little?

TOM: I am trying to be patient because I know you are disappointed and you obviously are too young to deal with it intelligently. Be reasonable.

DICK: Being reasonable ought to work both ways. You made a promise. *Again.*

TOM: I haven't time to argue. My time isn't my own. A man can't always do what he wants.

DICK: Depends on what he wants, doesn't it? Well, doesn't it?

TOM: You certainly are worked up over a little fishing trip!

DICK *(pleading):* Oh, Dad! It isn't just the fishing trip. It's *us.* Can't you see? *(Tom just looks at him and he turns away defeated.)* Oh, what's the use!

TOM *(briskly):* That's better. We'll go fishing soon. Now, that's a promise.

DICK *(trying again):* Dad, listen. I'm growing up. Soon I'll be away in college. If we can't talk—if we can't get together now, we never will.

(Phone rings.)

TOM: Hello. Yes, I'm hunting for them now.

DICK: Dad—

TOM: Okay. In a few minutes. *(Hangs up.)*

DICK: Dad—

11

Tom: Dick, be practical. I have responsibilities.

Dick: Even to your family. You don't know much about me, do you? What I do, what I think, where I go, my friends. Looks like you never will.

Tom *(already turning away, looking through papers):* Of course I know your friends. There's Betty and Jerry what's-his-name. Besides I trust you.

Dick: Because it's less trouble?

Tom: You must really want to pick a quarrel! You are old enough to act more like a man!

Dick: One of these days I'll *be* a man and have kids of my own. You want to know something? I may never take them near a church! They might get to be like you!

Tom: Don't be insolent!

Dick: You're so power-hungry you—

Tom *(shouting):* Richard, that is enough!

Dick *(throws up hands in defeat):* Okay, okay. I tried.

Tom: All right. That's better. Now, I promise we'll plan another day. Soon. Better clear that gear away.

(Tom goes interior. Dick sits on sofa, staring at floor. Tom returns, papers in hand, heads exterior.)

Tom: I found them. Tell your mother I'll be late. *(Exits.)*

(Dick looks at lure for a time, puts it in his pocket. Looks at gear, kicks it, jerks it up and takes to interior, slamming things around in anger.
Lights fade to show passage of time. Brief pause. When Martha enters, she seems to touch switch and lights come up. She goes interior, leaves purse and returns with notebook. She is making notations when Tom enters, evening paper in hand. Sinks wearily into a chair.

Martha *(absently):* Hello, dear. Why, Tom! I thought you and Dick went fishing?

12

TOM *(wearily):* I had to call it off. Representatives from Smith and from Brackett's were in town to talk contracts.

MARTHA: Did you get them signed?
TOM: Yes.
MARTHA: Good. My meeting went off like clockwork. Minnie Simpson had other ideas, as usual. But I convinced the others my ideas were best. Was Dick disappointed?

TOM: Yes. We came close to a real quarrel over it. He was pretty disrespectful. I'll have a talk with him when he cools down.

MARTHA *(lightly):* In a way, I understand. We really don't spend much time with him. But we never have, and he hasn't suffered.

TOM: Thanks to finding good baby-sitters when he was little. Well, he's no baby now. We both have a lot to do. He'll just have to accommodate. It's not easy to run my business and the church's too.

MARTHA: I know. But he said something unpleasant to me. He said *we* keep others from places of responsibility because *we* want to run things. Made us sound as if we were a couple of dictators!

TOM: My father would have had me out in the woodshed if I'd said to him some of the things Dick said to me today.

MARTHA: Somehow I wish you hadn't called off this trip. Oh, well. Where is Dick, by the way?

TOM: I haven't seen him since this afternoon. Perhaps next door with Betty.
BETTY *(exterior. Knocks, calls):* Anybody here?
MARTHA: In here, Betty. *(Betty enters.)*
BETTY: Hello. Dick here?
TOM *(opening paper):* Isn't he at your house?
BETTY: No. I saw him when I brought back his racket. Jerry and I played tennis. We're going bowling. Pat and Don are going, too. Jerry's picking me up at 7:30. Maybe Dick would like to go,

13

too. I want him to know what time.

MARTHA: You talked with him? Did he say where he was going?
BETTY: No, he didn't. *(Hesitantly.)* Mrs. Bradshaw—I don't mean to interfere, but—about Dick—

MARTHA: Yes?
BETTY: Haven't you noticed he acts, sort of funny?
MARTHA: Funny?
BETTY *(sadly):* Mrs. Bradshaw, don't you listen to him?
MARTHA: Out with it, Betty.
BETTY: Well, what he says and what he means aren't always the same. Like when I asked him earlier about going bowling, he yelled at me.

TOM: Yelled?
BETTY *(imitating his anger):* He said, "Why not? There's nothing *here!* Oh, I could go down and join the tables and chairs, but who cares?" He just yelled.

TOM *(coldly):* Dick was being childish. He was disappointed today and took it out on you. Don't give it a thought.

BETTY: He wasn't mad at me! Oh, well, okay if you say so. But *listen* to him more, Mr. Bradshaw, please! Tell Dick what Jerry said, will you?

MARTHA *(following her to exterior exit):* I will. Thank you, Betty. *(Betty leaves.)*

TOM: About what Betty said—
MARTHA: I think Dick is unhappy, Tom.
TOM: Now, why should he be unhappy? Dick has it too easy. A good home, spending money, everything.

MARTHA *(sits):* Apparently he doesn't think these are enough. He seems to have something on his mind—against *us.*

TOM *(settling back to his paper):* He's spoiled. He has too much. That's what.

14

(Dick enters, glances at parents, goes interior.)

MARTHA: Dick? Dick, come here a minute. Dick, did you hear me? *(He returns, stands silently at entrance.)* I have a message from Betty about bowling. Jerry will pick you up at 7:30.

DICK: I'm not going. *(Turns away.)*
TOM: Wait, Dick! Where were you all afternoon?
DICK: Out.
TOM: Richard!
DICK: Just out. Fooling around.
MARTHA: All this time?
TOM: Next time, leave a note so your mother won't worry.
DICK *(deliberately):* Did she?
MARTHA *(trying to ease tension):* I'm sorry supper isn't ready. I thought you'd both be fishing and hadn't planned—*(Realizes this isn't a good gambit.)* Well, I'll hurry and get something ready.

TOM: Not for me. Just a glass of milk. I think I'm getting an ulcer.
DICK: I'm not hungry. May I go to my room now?
TOM: Of course. *(Dick leaves.)* Martha, he's defying us.
MARTHA: Just like when he was little. Such a *trying* little boy! Remember?
TOM: I'll talk with him tomorrow. Let him alone tonight.

(A quick knock and voices exterior. Tom goes. The Alcotts enter, excited and talking at once.)

TOM: Henry! Agnes! Come in!
HENRY *(puffing a little):* We've come from the church.
AGNES *(horrified):* You should *see* it! Oh, *Martha!*
HENRY: Such a mess!
AGNES: When I think how it *looked.*

MARTHA: Whatever is the matter? Here, sit down. *(Agnes sits by her.)*
TOM: What's wrong, Henry?
HENRY: Vandals, that's what! *Vandals!* I should have gone for the police, but all I thought of was coming here, since you live so close.

MARTHA: But what is wrong?

AGNES: The new draperies in *shreds!* Knives, I guess. Oh, it is terrible—all around the choir and the baptistry and the windows—just *shreds!*

HENRY: And the rugs are slashed and ripped, and flower containers broken—

AGNES: And pews overturned!

HENRY: The new hymnals are torn and the pages are scattered everywhere—and the cover over the organ is all beaten and smashed.

AGNES: All I wanted to do was set out the choir music for *Sunday!*

TOM *(he and Martha had made horrified sounds of reaction):* Did you call the pastor?

HENRY: I couldn't call anyone. The study door was locked and the phone's in there. We came straight here.

TOM: Then he must be called at once. I'll do it. He can call the police.

(Tom makes several calls, keeping voice below dialogue.)

MARTHA: Why would anyone so desecrate a church? Must have been hoodlums from the south side.

AGNES: *Riff-raff!* I tell you, Martha, missions are good and all that, but when something like this happens, I wonder if it's *worth* it, building missions for people who don't *appreciate* them!

AGNES: Henry, you know good and well that no decently brought up child would deliberately tear up a *church.*

HENRY: We don't know it was a child.

AGNES: Oh, Henry, you know I don't mean a *child.* I—I mean a teenager, at least. It was probably a *gang.* They have *names,* you know. Juvenile delinquents! Really, Henry, there ought to be a *law!*

HENRY: There are. Several.

16

MARTHA: This is terrible. You found it?

AGNES: Yes. You see I forgot to leave the music for *Sunday* where we always *do*. I asked Henry to stop by the church. We turned on the lights, and there is *was*. Martha, it's awful. A mess! Those draperies, you worked so hard on them. What did they *cost?*

MARTHA: I hate to think about that.

AGNES: Well, they are a total loss. *Shredded.* You wouldn't believe it.

HENRY: Something odd. Look what was stuck there on the draperies —right there in plain sight. As if the vandals wanted us to find it. I wonder why? *(He pulls Dick's lure from his pocket. Martha takes it, shocked. Tom joins them but ignores the lure, never having seen it before.)*

AGNES: Martha, what's the matter?

MARTHA *(covering):* I—I'm shocked, that's all. About the church, I mean. *(Conceals lure.)*

HENRY *(sympathetically):* That church means a lot to you. Tom, what did the pastor say?

TOM: Dr. Harvey had me call the police while he went to the church. I called some of the deacons: Holmes, Smith, Letheridge. They're going over.

HENRY: This is a nasty business. I'm a good Christian, but I hope they catch those vandals and give them all the law allows!

AGNES: What will we do about tomorrow? The *services?*

TOM: When the police are through, I'm sure the janitors will make some kind of order out of the mess.

AGNES: Well, Henry, let's go home. I feel as if I've been through *something. (Rises.)* We'll see you in the morning.

HENRY *(importantly):* We ought to go back to talk to the police. They will expect us.

AGNES: Oh, all right.

HENRY: Tom, are you coming?

MARTHA: Go on, Tom.
TOM: Aren't you coming?
MARTHA: Later.
TOM: I won't be long.

(The three leave. Martha pulls out the lure, but conceals it again when Betty is heard exterior.)

BETTY: Dick! *(Enters.)* Oh, Mrs. Bradshaw! Mr. Bradshaw said it was all right to come in. Is Dick ready?

MARTHA: He isn't going.
BETTY: He, isn't sick, is he?
MARTHA: Why do you ask?
BETTY *(vaguely):* Oh, I don't know. He's all right?
MARTHA *(coldly):* He isn't sick. He's staying in tonight.
BETTY: Tell him we'll miss him. *(Leaves.)*
MARTHA *(looks at lure, goes to call Dick):* Dick!
DICK *(interior):* Yes?
MARTHA: Come here!
DICK: I'm in bed.
MARTHA: Put on a robe and come here! *(Silence.)* Do you hear me?
DICK: Oh, all right. *(In a moment, he enters.)* What is it?
MARTHA: Sit down, Richard. *Sit down! (He sits and she stands so her back is to exterior entrance.)* Where were you tonight?

DICK: Just around.
MARTHA: Where? Exactly!
DICK: Just around. Just fooling around.
MARTHA: Were you near the church? Were you near the church? Richard!
DICK: Maybe.
MARTHA *(Tom appears in exterior entrance. Listens):* How do you explain this? I saw this lure right here in this room today. Well, shall I draw the natural conclusion?

DICK *(defiantly):* No one's stopping you!
MARTHA: Dick, you *wanted* to be found out! That's why you left that lure, wasn't it?

TOM *(stepping in):* Why?

MARTHA: Tom! I thought you were at the church!

TOM: I took one look and decided to come back for you. Dick! *You* did *that?* Are you out of your mind? *(Dick is silent, Tom's temper flares.)* Richard, answer me! *(Silence. Tom grabs the front of Dick's robe and jerks him to his feet.)* Richard! Answer me! *(Silence. Tom shoves Dick back in the chair violently.)* Look at his face! Someone from a bad environment, and underprivileged kid from the slums, yes, I could understand that! But *not my son!* You've had everything! A good home—

DICK: Is it?

TOM: What did you say? What did you *say? Answer me!*

DICK *(stands defiantly):* Is this a good home? Is it even a home? That's what I said!

TOM *(furious): You ungrateful*—

DICK *(shouting):* Well, *is it?*

TOM *(slaps him across face):* I ought to thrash you within an inch of your life!

DICK *(unresisting):* Why don't you? Would it make you feel better? Make you a bigger man before everyone? Would it?

TOM *(furious):* Don't tempt me!

DICK: I might be able to stop you. I'm almost strong enough, but I won't. The way I figure it, that'll just about even the score for the church. I'll gladly pay for the pleasure!

MARTHA: Richard!

DICK *(turning on her):* Yes, pleasure. You should have seen me. I didn't know I could undo so fast what you had done. All by myself!

TOM *(jerking him around by the shoulder):* Listen to me! Just because you're my son, don't think I'll cover for you on this! I have an obligation to the church.

DICK *(pulling away):* Yes, the church! Let's not forget the church for

19

one little moment. Let's bow down and worship it, every single brick and plank and curtain in the place!

MARTHA: Richard!
DICK: And all those people looking up to you so admiringly, patting you on the back and saying how wonderful you are.

MARTHA: Stop it!
DICK: And how devoted to the church! *Now* they can add, "After all they've been through with that son of theirs!" Oh, it will take some time to live down the disgrace but I'm counting on you both to do it! Think how you'll enjoy having everyone come around to say how noble and self-sacrificing you are!

TOM: Shut up!
DICK: You'll just lap it up! Makes me sick!
MARTHA: After what you've done? Talking that way about people who love the Lord?
DICK: I bet the Lord gets tired of hearing people say they love him while they sit out the duration, turning everything over to you! Power hogs!

TOM: I've *heard enough!*
DICK: You couldn't get away with it if people didn't let you. I don't believe they *do* love the Lord. And what's more I don't believe you do either. What you really love is power.

TOM *(grabs his robe and shakes him hard):* Be quiet! You act as if *you* are innocent and *we* are guilty! God forgive you!

DICK *(jerking away):* Don't drag God into this! I'm not sorry! I don't want to be forgiven!

TOM: You can't talk that way and stay in this house!
DICK *(faces them from interior exit):* That's fine with me! Don't you want to call the police? Go ahead. I'll finish dressing so the neighbors won't be shocked by seeing a Bradshaw dragged out in his pajamas! *(Exits.)*

20

MARTHA *(sinking to sofa):* The neighbors! Oh, Tom! How could this have happened?

TOM: It is not our fault.

MARTHA: But people will say.

TOM: We are not responsible for what Dick has done. Even if it is the fashion to blame the parents for what their children do.

MARTHA: If there were a reason.

TOM: There is not. I don't understand it either.

MARTHA: Must you call the police?

TOM: Certainly! And the pastor, too. I hope to heaven he'll have the sense to see we aren't responsible. It is going to be bad, Martha. *(Goes to exit, calls.)* Dick! Are you dressed?

DICK *(interior):* Almost.

TOM: Then come here!

DICK *(after pause, entering, pulling on jacket):* I'm ready.

MARTHA: Sit down, Richard.

DICK: Did you call the police?

TOM: Not yet.

DICK: My tennis racket that Betty borrows is upstairs. Let her keep it. She might want to play and I won't be using it.

TOM: Tennis rackets? With all this facing us? *(Knock is heard.)* Now what? *(To Dick, suspiciously.)* The church was the only place you visited tonight, I hope? *(Goes to exterior exit.)* Oh, Betty.

BETTY: Mr. Bradshaw, I heard about the church.

TOM: Already?

BETTY: Stan Holmes came to the bowling alley and told us. Have they any idea who did it?

TOM *(heavy sarcasm):* Suppose, just suppose I told you it was Dick. Would you be surprised?

MARTHA: Oh, Tom!

TOM *(angrily):* The whole town will know by morning. And by the

21

time the papers get through with the story, the name of Bradshaw will—

MARTHA: Dick! Why didn't you think of us?

DICK: I did. A lot.

MARTHA: Then how could you have done it?That church is our whole life! Aside from his business, your father gives all his time, and I practically live there! We're never home.

DICK: I know.

BETTY: Oh, Dick!

MARTHA: Do you really understand?

DICK: Yes, I think I do—at last.

TOM: When I think of all the advantages you've had. This is a fine way to repay us.

DICK: Yes, father.

MARTHA: I don't think you do see what you've done to us!

DICK: Oh—I see.

TOM: I had a full schedule for next week. Now—

MARTHA: I, too. Oh! We'll have to resign from everything! This whole thing is simply awful. I feel like crying.

DICK: Go ahead. But don't pretend it's for me.

BETTY *(goes to Dick):* Dick, I'm sorry!

TOM: Is that all you have to say, Betty?

BETTY *(quickly):* Well, I *am* sorry for Dick!

TOM *(angrily):* For *Dick?* That's hardly what I expected from you! Unless—you know him pretty well, don't you Betty? *(Harshly.)* Is this the first time? What about those schools last summer? Answer me, Dick!

DICK: You have to *ask?*

TOM: Answer the question. Have you done this before?

DICK: No.

MARTHA: Why the church, Dick?

DICK: You wouldn't understand.

MARTHA: Try me!

BETTY *(insisting): Tell* them.

DICK *(looks at Betty, searching for words):* I—I know now I was wrong.

MARTHA: I should hope so!

DICK: Betty, I just found out. It could have been anything else. Business, a club. Charity.

BETTY: Politics?

DICK: Yes.

MARTHA: I don't understand a word you're saying!

DICK: I've been thinking for a long time it was the church's fault. Even—even when I'd remember how I loved it when I was a little kid. Singing those songs and hearing—hearing those stories about Jesus. Then, it wasn't the same. And I—I couldn't see how God could be in a building that took so much.

TOM *(impatiently):* What is all this hogwash? What are you saying?

BETTY *(urgently):* Go on, Dick.

DICK *(stumbling through):* Partly it was, I wanted so for us to be a real family. And I thought the church was to blame. So I came to hate it. And wanted to smash it. Even tonight I still thought it was the church.

TOM: Martha, you may be able to make sense out of this but I can't.

DICK: I said you wouldn't understand. At least I found out in the last few minutes that it wasn't the church at all. Nor God. I'm glad. I—missed God. It felt so lonely.

BETTY *(urgently):* Dick, whatever happens, keep remembering I care!

DICK: I'll remember!

MARTHA: Betty, don't be dramatic. You were here this afternoon, weren't you? What happened?

BETTY: Nothing. We just talked.

MARTHA *(incredulously):* It *couldn't* have been—the *fishing* trip?

TOM: The fishing trip! Martha, nobody would believe such a thing!

BETTY: I would.

TOM: So you think it's normal for a fifteen-year-old boy to destroy property because his father didn't take him fishing?

BETTY: It was sort of the last straw.

TOM: Dick has been raised in that church. He's had a good Christian home and parents who taught him right from wrong. We gave him everything.

BETTY *(defiantly)*: No, he hasn't! He's had nothing! Not really. Like a tinkling cymbal. Oh, it's all mixed up!

TOM: I think so. What are you trying to say? Go ahead and say it.

DICK: I said they wouldn't understand.

TOM: I'll be the judge of that. Go on, Betty.

BETTY: I—I can't.

TOM: Why not?

BETTY: No matter what I said, you wouldn't believe it wasn't Dick's fault.

TOM: I certainly wouldn't! If you two are a sample of the thinking of your generation—well, I'm not surprised at the crime rate.

DICK *(to Betty)*: Don't try.

TOM: How do you think the police will take it when I tell them you did all that because I wouldn't go fishing?

MARTHA *(worried)*: This will change so many things.

TOM: It's going to cost us something and don't you forget it. Under the law I'm responsible for the damage you did.

DICK: I'll pay you back!

TOM *(scornfully)*: You couldn't pay that much back for years!

DICK *(angrily)*: I'll pay you someday.

TOM: I'll tell you this. You mother and I have discussed it several times before but now this settles it. *You* are going into a military school somewhere. A place where they have real discipline. That's what you need.

BETTY: Oh, Dick!

DICK: It doesn't matter.

MARTHA: Tom, I agree. The sooner the better.

TOM: The police will have a say. But since this is a first offense and we are assuming financial responsibility, it shouldn't be long before he can leave.

MARTHA *(thinking):* A school not too near. I'll look them up. He ought to stay away long enough for people to forget.

BETTY *(pleading):* What about Dick? Doesn't he have any say? Don't you want him here?

DICK: Now you know, Betty.
BETTY *(to him alone):* Oh, Dick! Oh, Dick.
MARTHA *(coldly):* We have to be sensible, Betty.
TOM: You are too young to understand.
MARTHA *(brightening):* Tom! If we get this settled quickly—all of it—maybe we won't have to resign.

TOM *(righteously):* Christians should do their duty, no matter the personal cost. It's always best to get unpleasant things over. I'll call the police. And, Martha, when we talk about it, let's play it down. *(They go to the phone.)* We must forgive an uncontrollable impulse that came over the boy and we are making things right and doing our duty by placing him under close discipline—how does that sound? You know, I think this will work out. *(Dials, as Martha returns to Dick and Betty. He continues under dialogue.)* Is this the police station? This is—

MARTHA: Betty, you'd better go home. Your parents won't want you involved. Dick, you heard your father?

DICK: I heard.
MARTHA: Now, you straighten up, young man! We have enough to put up with right now without your surliness!

DICK: Yes—mother.
MARTHA *(coldly):* We expect your full cooperation.
DICK: Yes—mother.

(Betty turns away to hide tears.)

MARTHA: Betty, don't be silly! This is no time for crying.

DICK: Don't cry.

MARTHA: The sooner we get you away from here, the better for all of us.

DICK: Yes—mother. *(Betty is crying into her hands. Dick puts his arm around her.)* I'll be all right, Betty. I'll be *all right.*

MARTHA: Well, that's better! You sound as if you might grow up at last.

DICK *(softly):* Oh, I did. Mother. I *did.* Tonight.

(Tom hangs up receiver. He and Martha look at Dick, puzzled at his tone. Betty hides her face against Dick weeping.)

THE END

LOVE TRIUMPHANT
or
SHERIFF, ARREST THAT MAN!

This melodrama is set in the time of when automobiles were a novelty, villains were always unmasked, and true love always emerged triumphant. The *PLACE* is the yard at the Bascom farm. A door left back leads to the house, the left exit to town, and the right exit to the barn. Upstage center is a bench. Downstage far right is an inadequate small branch or bush in a can, labeled "bush."

The *CHORUS* includes any number of persons, located in the audience or backstage. Because of the *CHORUS*, this play may be used as a recreational activity for an entire organization. Besides the *CHORUS*, the cast includes:

NEWT BASCOM—hearty middle-aged farmer, in overalls and straw hat.

LUTIE BASCOM—his middle-aged wife, ambitious for her daughter, in long gingham dress and "cook" apron.

VINNIE BASCOM—their daughter, about 18, romantic, simple. Wears long gingham dress, heavy work shoes, pigtails.

ELMER WILKINS—her clumsy, good-hearted, bucolic swain from the next farm. Let him wear too-small overalls, too-large brogans, oversized straw hat.

UTTLEY HUNTINGDON—the villain, a city slicker and crook. He might wear a duster, goggles, and cap over a frock coat and spats. Black mustache and black slicked-down hair.

BEATRICE HUNTINGDON—his unwanted, betrayed wife. Let her wear traveling costume of the day and large plumed hat.

SHERIFF HIGGINS—the law. Wears Stetson, star, and guns. Has a heavy mustache.

Note: all the acting is overdone. For scene changes, simply lower and raise the lights.

SCENE 1—Morning

CHORUS: Little did the Bascoms suspect what fate would bring to them this beautiful summer morning! All is peaceful and quiet on the Bascom farm. If Vinnie Bascom knew what the day would bring, would she come out that door? But she doesn't suspect, so here she comes!

(VINNIE enters from house, noisily clomps over to bench and flops down to read a book. In a moment, Elmer enters left, elaborately tip-toeing. VINNIE pretends not to see him until he is near, then acts startled.)

VINNIE: Oh, El-l-lmer! You skeered me!

ELMER *(sits beside her, bashfully):* Aw, now, Vinnie, I didn't go to skeer ye, not fer nuthin'! Whut ye readin' outta that there book?

VINNIE *(dreamily):* "The Loves of the Countess"—that's hit's name. Hit's so thrillin' an' romantic. *(Sighs gustily.)* My sakes, whut it mus' be like to wear all them fancy gowns an' sparkly jewels, an' flowers an' doo-dads! Hit'd shore purty-up a body.

ELMER *(bashfully):* Well—uh—well, *I* think yore purty 'thouten no doo-dads, Vinnie!

VINNIE *(with pleasure):* Oh, El-l-lmer! Yore jist a-funnin' me.

ELMER: 'Tis so! Why the sun a-shinin' on yore hair makes little goldy lights—jist like ol' Bess after a rub-down! An'—an'—(Lamely.) Wal, ye do look purty!

VINNIE (preening herself): Wal, thank ye kindly, Elmer, I must say. (Rises and walks about illustrating.) But I shore do wisht I could have one o' them long dresses with a swishy train, an'—an' diamonds in my hair, an' a iv'ry fan from Chiny—an' go to one o' them big re-ceptions, like the books allus tell about, with han'some men all dressed up fancy an' wearin' colog-ney! I bet they all smell good!

CHORUS (draw "smell" in noisily and then exhale noisily): Ah-h-h-h.

ELMER (defensively): Well, I cain't hep it becuz pigs an' cows don't smell like colog-ney! When I git to town Sattiday, I'll git me a haircut an' have ol' Jim Foster put some of that there Bay Rum on me!

VINNIE (apologetically, sits): No, El-l-lmer, I ain't sayin' ye don't smell good.

ELMER (nervously): Vinnie—Vinnie, I come over special this mornin' —I come over special to ask ye somethin' special.

VINNIE (innocently): Whut did ye want to ask me, Elmer? Somethin' yore Maw wants to borry?

ELMER: Naw, it ain't that. Maw don't want nuthin'.

VINNIE: Mebbe hit's about that there candy-pull over to Simpson's next week, an' ye wanta beau me? Oh, Elmer, ye don't have to ask me special about the Simpsons.

ELMER (frustrated): Naw, I don't wanna ask ye—wal, o' course, I wanna beau ye to Simpson's, but that ain't what I come special fer! I—I—

VINNIE (interrupting): Oh, I know! Hit's the all-day speakin' Sunday! O' course—

ELMER (jumps to his feet): Vinnie Bascom! Yore jist a-befuddlin' me! I don't want ye to go with me to the speakin'—wal, I do, too!

29

(Shouting.) But that ain't whut I come special fer! Whut I come special fer wuz to ask ye to marry-up with me!

CHORUS *(romantically):* A-a-ah!

VINNIE *(pertly):* Wal, why din't ye jist up an' say so then? Stidda all that talkin' aroun'!

ELMER: I tried to! But ye—oh-h-h, Vinnie, willya?

VINNIE *(coyly):* Oh, Elmer, this is so sudden.

ELMER *(indignantly):* Sudden? Vinnie Bascom, ye bin a-knowin' fer a long time how my heart wuz jist a-bustin' fer ye. *(Takes her hand.)* Vinnie, will ye marry-up with me? Oh, I know I gotta git some money. I bin savin' fer a right long time. I got me a hunnert an' twelve dollars an' thirty-one cents!

VINNIE *(impressed):* Well!

ELMER: We could be wed in less'n a year fer shore. Please, Vinnie.

VINNIE *(primly):* Wal, now, Elmer, I gotta have some thinkin' time. It ain't the money part that's hinderin', but a girl has gotta think a perposal over. Tain't as if'n hit happened ever' day! First off, a girl's gotta know her feller real good.

ELMER: Why, Vinnie Bascom! We bin a-livin' next door to each other since you wuz born.

VINNIE: But we're growed up, an' hit's kinda different. Now, don't ye git yore dander up, Elmer. I'll let ye know soon's ever I make up my mind. Gittin' married ain't somethin' ye jist up an' rush into like!

CHORUS: Poor Elmer! Patience, friend!

(NEWT BASCOM enters from barn, carrying a pail.)

NEWT *(heartily):* Howdy there, Elmer! Come over to court Vinnie a spell? If'n ye ain't got enough to do over to yore place, I kin use a extry hand here! All my boys wuz a girl! *(Laughs at own wit.)* How's yore folks?

30

ELMER *(glumly):* Oh, I reckon they're peart, Mr. Bascom.

NEWT *(cheerfully):* Hens ain't a-layin' so good right now. Guess hit's too hot fer 'em. Better git these here eggs in to Lutie. She's pinin' to make a sweetcake fer dinner. Be proud fer ye to stay, Elmer.

ELMER: No, thank ye, kindly, Mr. Bascom, but hit's right neighborly of ye to ask.

NEWT *(at house door):* Lutie! Lutie, Elmer's here. See ye later, Elmer. *(Goes in.)*

ELMER: Wal, if'n ye ain't goin' to give me no answer today, guess I better git along home. Paw wants to finish plowin' the west forty today.

(LUTIE BASCOM comes to house door.)

LUTIE: Howdy there, Elmer. Yore folks feelin' peart?

ELMER: Yes ma'am.

LUTIE: Ye go tell yer Maw I got a new *re*-ceet fer chocklit cake. I'm a-goin' to bake up a big 'un this mornin'. Tell yer Maw I'll have Vinnie fetch her some. Now, mind ye tell her! *(Re-enters house.)*

VINNIE: Maw sets a heap o' store by her cakes.

(UTTLEY HUNTINGDON enters left.)

CHORUS: Enter the villain of the play! *(Hiss.)*

UTTLEY *(with a courtly bow, speaking in an affected tone):* Ah, good morning, young lady! *(With a sneer.)* Good morning, boy!

BOTH *(VINNIE eagerly, ELMER antagonistic):* Mornin'.

UTTLEY: I am in difficulty. A part has broken on my automobile.

VINNIE: Autymobile? I ain't never been in a autymobile in my whole entire life!

ELMER: Ye mean ye rid out cheer in a autymobile?

UTTLEY: It's stopped now just down the road. I wonder if I might hire a buggy into town so that I can order a part sent from the city?

VINNIE: Elmer, fetch Paw!

ELMER *(calling out before he moves a step):* Mr. Bascom! Mr. Bascom! *(Reluctantly he leaves and goes into the house, still calling.)* Mr. Bascom, Vinnie wants ye!

UTTLEY *(suavely):* Vinnie! What a charming and unusual name for a charming and unusual young lady! *(He leers, smoothes mustache, wiggles eyebrows.)*

VINNIE *(flustered):* Hit's short fer Vanilla.

UTTLEY *(looking about inquisitively):* A charming and delightful farm, this. And prosperous, too. Hmmmm. Will you have a share of it some day?

VINNIE: Why, I'll heir it all. Paw 'n' Maw ain't got no more kids. Jist me. They's more'n five hunnerd acres o' good land here!

UTTLEY: How interesting. You are not married?

VINNIE *(shyly):* Not yit. Elmer—*(Points to house.)* *He's* Elmer—asked me to wed him. He done it this mornin'. I ain't give him my answer yit.

UTTLEY: Elmer may be a worthy young man, but, you, my dear, are lovely.

VINNIE: I am?

UTTLEY: Indeed yes. Far too lovely to be wasted on a country bumpkin.

VINNIE: Wal, now! Elmer's *nice!*

UTTLEY: Undoubtedly. *(Draws near and looks soulfully into her eyes.)* But, Vinnie, a girl with your beauty and charm should not be hidden in the backwoods. Why, you should be seen in great concert halls, at the theater, at the opera. You should dress in lovely gowns and fabulous gems! A jewel of nature, such as you, needs a proper setting. Now, if I were Elmer, lucky chap, I would take you away with me to the city where all the delights of city life could be yours!

VINNIE: Ye would? In a autymobile?

UTTLEY: Indeed I would. I live in that world and I would be more than happy to show my world to you, and to show such a fair flower to my world, if I were Elmer.

VINNIE: Elmer never did say nuthin' like that!

CHORUS: Be careful, Vinnie! This is a snake in human form. He's after your father's property. Beware! Beware!

(NEWT, LUTIE and ELMER come from house.)

NEWT: Howdy, stranger! Elmer here tells me you got a autymobile broke down clost by.

UTTLEY: Uttley Huntingdon at your service, sir! *(Deep bow.)* Yes, I must get to town and put up at a local hotel while I have a duplicate part sent out from the city. Meanwhile I'd like to get my machine to shelter and off the road. Perhaps we might push it to your place?

NEWT *(holding out his hand)*: Our name is Bascom. This here's Miz Bascom an' my daughter, Vinnie. An' this here's Elmer Wilkins, Vinnie's feller. Shore we'll push yore machine to our barn, won't we, Elmer? Let's go. *(They all leave left.)*

CHORUS: Poor Elmer! Even now his be-dazzled little Vinnie is being won away from him! Poor Elmer. The farm looks peaceful, doesn't it? But a human storm is about to break, all because of that villain, Uttley Huntingdon! By now, they are pushing the car to the barn: the unsuspecting Bascoms, the bewildered Elmer, and the sly Uttley. Sly, because he has wangled an invitation to stay at the farm. Stay until the broken part can be replaced, that is. Oh, fatal decision! Little do these simple people suspect the villain for what he is, nor realize the danger to their darling, and their acres!

(All return from the right. VINNIE and LUTIE lead, followed by NEWT and UTTLEY. ELMER drags in last, carrying UTTLEY'S suitcase.)

NEWT: That oughta get her outa the rain. Elmer, fetch Mr. Hunting-don's valise up to the attic room. *(To UTTLEY.)* That there machine is mighty fancy. Cost plenty, I daresay. Doubt if'n them things'll ever replace the horse, though! *(ELMER goes into the house reluctantly.)*

LUTIE: I 'spect you menfolks is gittin' hungry. Me an' Vinnie'll git dinner on in no time a-tall. Set yourselves an' rest a spell. Jist you come along, Vinnie. *(They go inside.)*

UTTLEY: This is most gracious of you, Mr. Bascom. I hope it isn't too much trouble. I do need to send for that part right away, however.

NEWT: Hit ain't no trouble. Proud to hev ye. My womenfolks'll enjoy fussin' over company. *(ELMER returns.)* Here comes Elmer back. Hit wouldn't surprise me none if'n Elmer wasn't willin' to take yer message in to town. That right, Elmer?

ELMER *(fervently)*: Hit'll pleasure me to take the message—an' help ye git away sooner!

CHORUS: That's telling him, Elmer!

NEWT: Jist you write it out an' Elmer'll take hit right down to the post office.

UTTLEY: Post office?

NEWT: They's a tellygraph right there! Oh, we got city ways!

UTTLEY *(writes on piece of paper from his pocket)*: This ought to do it. *(Hands paper to ELMER.)* There, boy. Thank you.

NEWT: Wal, we'd best be gittin' in to dinner. Now, you go on Elmer.

(The two men go inside, ELMER off left. Lights dim briefly then full again.)

SCENE 2—that evening after supper

34

CHORUS: It's evening. *Two* meals and several hours of smooth talk later, smooth talk by Uttley Huntingdon, that is.

(LUTIE comes out carrying a paper fan. Sits on bench. UTTLEY joins her.)

UTTLEY: Enjoying the cool of the evening, I see. What a superb cook you are, Mrs. Bascom. Never have I tasted better. Not even in the finest restaurants in New York.

LUTIE: You spend much time in New York, Mr. Huntingdon?

UTTLEY *(importantly):* Ah, yes, indeed. Have I mentioned that I am an investment broker?

LUTIE: If'n ye did, I ain't heerd it.

UTTLEY: The center of the stock market trading is in New York, you know. Fascinating city, New York. If I may say so, Mrs. Bascom, your daughter is as lovely as any lady in the city. It is a shame she cannot show city dwellers what charm can come from these rural areas.

LUTIE: Thank ye kindly, Mr. Huntingdon. Vinnie favors her great-aunt Flora. *(Lowers voice.)* We don't say hit much 'cause Flora was the black sheep of the family. *(Looks around to see if anyone is listening, stage whisper.)* She—she married a *Methodist!* *(Note: substitute other denomination from your own.)*

UTTLEY *(pretended shock): No!*

LUTIE *(sighs):* Yes, she did, an' went out to Californey an' none o' us ever seen her again! Ye say yore a *in*-vestment broker? Jist whut's that?

CHORUS: Oh-oh!

UTTLEY: Oh, I take money that people want invested. I invest it for them in stocks and bonds, in that way their money earns more money.

LUTIE: I 'spose hit takes rich folks to *in*-vest money.

UTTLEY: No, indeed, Mrs. Bascom. Why, you could be an investor if you had a small sum, say, put away somewhere.

LUTIE *(looking around):* Would—would a body's husband hev to know 'bout a—a *in*-vestment?

UTTLEY: Not if she didn't want him to know. Why? Do you have some money you would like to invest, Mrs. Bascom? I would be glad to take care of it for you.

CHORUS: He would, too!

LUTIE: Mr. Huntingdon, Newt don't know hit, but I got a little money laid by in a ol' silver pitcher on the top shelf in the pantry. I bin a-savin' hit fer Vinnie's weddin' finery, but a—a *in*-vestment— wal, mebbe I could fancy her up real good. I'll go fetch hit. You jist sit right there! And not a word to Newt!

UTTLEY: Oh, I'll not tell him, dear lady! *(She goes inside.)*

CHORUS: And he won't. The villain is making himself known in his true colors at last. Did you see the covetous look on his face at the mention of money? Poor Lutie. The villain will take her money and leave her disillusionment. Someone's coming! It's Vinnie. Poor little innocent Vinnie is about to be ensnared in that spider's web. Stay away, Vinnie! Stay away! *(VINNIE enters.)*

VINNIE: Oh, howdy, Mr. Huntingdon.

UTTLEY *(meets her, takes her hand, speaks intimately):* Lovely lady, call me Uttley. And may I call you Vinnie, Vinnie?

VINNIE *(embarrassed):* Yep! I mean, o' course. Ever'body does 'cause hit's my name.

UTTLEY: Let's go walking in the meadow, to see the stars and commune with nature.

(NEWT and LUTIE enter.)

NEWT: We wuz jist comin' out to set a spell. Where ye off to?

VINNIE *(happily):* Mr. Huntingdon an' me is goin' communin'. We'll be down in the medder. *(LUTIE has slipped something into UTTLEY'S hand.)*

LUTIE: Jist you young folks run along. Newt, leave 'em be. Come set an' rest a spell.

(UTTLEY and VINNIE leave right. LUTIE sits and begins to fan. NEWT sits beside her.)

NEWT: "Communin'." Whut's that?

LUTIE: Don't be countrified, Newt. Vinnie jist meant her an' Mr. Huntingdon is goin' walkin' in the medder, lookin' at the stars.

NEWT: Whyn't she say so, then? Puttin' on airs. 'Sides, the medder ain't no higher 'n' here. I ain't shore I trust this city feller, Lutie!

LUTIE *(agitated)*: Now, you listen here, Newt Bascom! This here is the first city *gentleman* Vinnie ever seen. Besides he's a rich investment broker an' if'n he wuz to cotton to our Vinnie an' marry-up with her, she could live like one o' them queens. You know she's bound to marry someone like Elmer if'n she stays on the farm!

CHORUS: N-o-o, Lutie! Uttley Huntingdon will break your little girl's heart! He'll steal your money and take the farm some day. While Elmer—'neath that rough exterior beats a heart of purest gold, however unrefined!

NEWT: Elmer's all right, Maw. He won't win no prizes, but leastways a feller knows where he's at with Elmer. But that Huntingdon feller uses sich big words. Did you understan' whut he wuz a-talkin' about at supper?

LUTIE: No, but hit jist suited my listenin'. Don't he soun' elegant? Oh, Newt, if our little girl could jist wed up with a feller like—*(Looks left.)* Wal, I do believe that's Elmer a-comin' up the road. Honest, that boy's bin underfoot all day!

NEWT: Guess he's jist green-jealous o' that Huntingdon feller. Howdy, there, Elmer! Bin some time since I seen ye, boy!

ELMER *(embarrassed):* Howdy Mr. Bascom, Mrs. Bascom. Uh—uh— Vinnie here?

LUTIE: Wal, now, Elmer, since ye ask, Vinnie *ain't* here. Leastwise, not jist *right* here. Not right now. She's a-communin' with Mr. Uttley Huntingdon down in the medder. 'Pears like yore nose is kinda outa joint, don't hit, boy?

ELMER: Miz Bascom, I don't trust that feller! Leastwise not around Vinnie!

LUTIE: Now Elmer, you jist got a jealousy fer him. Don't ye go sayin' nothin' agin Mr. Huntingdon to Vinnie! He's the first feller she ever seen who's got class. Not that you ain't a real nice boy an' all that, but, Elmer, you gotta admit you ain't in Uttley Huntingdon's class.

CHORUS: How true, how true!

NEWT *(rises, stretches, yawns loudly):* Well, Maw, reckin I'd better go fasten up the barn fer the night. *(Off right.)*

LUTIE: Yes, an' I better go redd up them dishes if we gonna git some sleep tonight. *(Pointedly.)* You leavin', Elmer?

ELMER: If hit don't never-you-mind, Miz Bascom, I'll set till Vinnie an' Mr. Huntingdon git back.

LUTIE: Wal, I'm shore I don't mind if ye want to make a silly o' yourself! *(She enters house. ELMER sits and mopes.)*

CHORUS: Love, how cruel it is! Here is this faithful, not bright, but *faithful* heart, broken because of one flighty girl. Brace up, Elmer! The truth will eventually out. Be patient and bide your time.

(VINNIE and UTTLEY return, arm in arm, not pleased to see ELMER.)

VINNIE: Oh! Howdy, Elmer.

UTTLEY: The bucolic swain back again! My dear fellow, don't you know the night air is bad for growing boys? Besides, I'm sure you need your rest.

VINNIE: Yes, Elmer, I'm shore ye've had a hard day, tryin' to git the plowin' done in between comin' over here seven times! We'll jist bid ye good night!

ELMER *(rising and going right):* Wal, aw right! G'night! But I'm goin' out to the barn an' say g'night to Mr. Bascom, I am!

CHORUS *(as ELMER leaves):* Don't let them run you off, Elmer!

UTTLEY: Come, my dear. Let us sit on this bench and talk. I have something very important to say to you.

VINNIE *(coyly, as they sit):* All right—*Uttley!*

UTTLEY *(clasps her hand to his breast):* If it hadn't been for a broken part in an automobile I would never have met you, my sweet! How strange are the ways of fate.

CHORUS: How strange, indeed.

VINNIE: I ain't never knowed nobody like you, Mr. Huntingdon. I mean Uttley! The fellers 'round here is more like Elmer.

UTTLEY: My dear, it pains me deeply to think of your future here on this farm. However lovely a spot it is, it is not the life for you.

VINNIE: Hit ain't?

UTTLEY: No, Vinnie. You are meant for greater fields.

VINNIE: Wal, our farm has purty big fields itself!

UTTLEY: That is not what I meant, my dear. You should be in the city, wearing all the beautiful clothes you could ask for, and having all the lovely times such a charming girl ought to have, with someone who admires, oh, let me be bold and say it! With someone who *loves* you, Vinnie! *(He hugs her close.)*

CHORUS *(moans):* O-o-oh!

UTTLEY: Someone who loves you more than life itself. Vinnie, dear, do I shock you with my boldness? *(Releases her momentarily.)*

39

VINNIE: I reckon not! *(Proudly.)* This here's my *second* perposal today? Ye are perposin', ain't ye? *(She gets closer.)*

UTTLEY: But of course! How could you think otherwise? Vinnie, my dear, could you bring yourself to marry me some day?

VINNIE: Wal, now, I don't see why not. 'Specially with you talkin' 'bout all them city doin's. Sounds mighty temptin', mighty temptin'. But I gotta be sure ye ain't makin' a *mis*-take, Uttley. Ye never seen me 'fore today.

UTTLEY: But, Vinnie, you have charms of which you are utterly unaware.

CHORUS: Five hundred acres of good land!

VINNIE: Ye shore kin sweettalk, Uttley! Hit jist pleasures me to set an' listen to ye.

UTTLEY: Vinnie, I have obligations in the city, and when my automobile is ready to travel, I must leave. It ought to be ready by tomorrow night. I'll plan to get away the next morning. I wish you were going with me.

VINNIE: Oh, Paw wouldn't never hear to that! He wouldn't let us get married-up so sudden like. *(Sits away from him, agitated.)*

UTTLEY *(impetuously):* Why tell him? Why should we have to wait when we are so sure? Why can't you have the things now that you deserve? You could, if it weren't for your father.

VINNIE: Wal, I jist don't know no way o' gettin' 'round hit.

UTTLEY: We could elope.

VINNIE: *E*-lope? Why there ain't never been a *e*-lopement in our whole family!

UTTLEY: Perhaps no one in your family has ever been as beautiful as you—and as tempting. I can't bear to go away and leave you. Ah, Vinnie, think how marvelous would be our life together!

CHORUS: Don't listen to him, Vinnie! He's leading you on!

VINNIE *(hesitates):* I—I don't know.

UTTLEY: Don't stop to think! Say you will elope with me. We can be married at the county seat on the way to the city.

CHORUS: Don't trust him, Vinnie, or you'll regret it! Little do you know what a villain he is! *(Hiss.)*

VINNIE *(decides):* Wal . . . I guess so.
UTTLEY *(clasping her to him):* Oh, my lovely Vinnie! You will never regret this, I promise you. Now, you must go in quickly before your mother begins to wonder. Tomorrow night, when the automobile is ready and everyone has gone to sleep, we will fly away together. Listen! I hear someone coming! *(Moves away from her.)*

(LUTIE calls as she comes from house. NEWT and ELMER enter right.)

LUTIE *(calling):* Vinneee! Vinnie, hit's time you wuz a-comin' in.
VINNIE *(goes to door):* Yes, Maw, I'm comin'.
NEWT: Goin' to bed, Vinnie? Wal, g'night. Say g'night to Elmer.
VINNIE *(rudely):* Good-night, Elmer! *(To UTTLEY in a different tone.)* Good-night, Mr. Huntingdon. I hope ye sleep good.

UTTLEY *(formally):* Good-night, Miss Vinnie. Thank you for your solicitude. Good-night, Mrs. Bascom. May I tell you again how your hospitality has lifted my spirits. It has contributed greatly to my comfort.

CHORUS: And it sure will in the future if this villain has his way!
NEWT: G'night, Elmer. Thank ye fer givin' me a hand with the chores.

(Elmer walks left despondently. All others into the house, as lights dim momentarily for end of scene.)

SCENE 3—the next morning

CHORUS: The night hours pass and the day dawns, the final, fatal day.

41

(ELMER comes from left, hears someone, conceals himself behind the "bush." UTTLEY enters from house, looking for VINNIE, who enters from right, carrying a pail.)

UTTLEY *(in a low tone):* Ah, there you are. The part for the machine has arrived in the mail buggy. I shall have it repaired by late afternoon. Sometime during the day, when no one sees you, you'd better bring your suitcase out and put it in the automobile. Just think! When everyone is asleep, we will go away together, my little Vinnie! *(Kisses her hand.)* Now, we must get busy. Act as natural as you can today, so that no one will suspect.

VINNIE *(nervously):* Hit's gonna be kinda hard. I ain't never e-loped before.

(UTTLEY leaves left. VINNIE enters house. LUTIE comes out with pan of beans to snap and sits on bench. ELMER steps from concealment in agitation.)

LUTIE *(heartily):* G'mornin', Elmer!
ELMER: Shhh! Miz Bascom, be quiet!
LUTIE: What ails ye, boy? Whut's the matter?
ELMER *(stammering):* M-Miz Bascom, I don't hardly—hardly know how to tell ye this. M-Miz Bascom, I jist heerd Vinnie an', an' that Huntingdon feller talkin'—an' Miz Bascom—Miz Bascom—

LUTIE *(irritated):* Wal, fer land's sakes, Elmer, spit hit out! Don't jist stand there gawpin'!

ELMER: Miz Bascom, him an' Vinnie is planning to e-lope! *(LUTIE is shocked.)* Yes'm, soon's ever you folks is asleep, he's a-takin' her to the city! He's gonna git the weddin' done at the county seat and they goin' in his autymobile to the city! *(LUTIE'S emotions change to speculation and then acceptance.)* Miz Bascom, we gotta stop 'em!

LUTIE: I like to know whut fer? So's she can stay here an' marry up with you, Elmer Wilkins?

42

ELMER: Yes'm!

LUTIE: Elmer, if ye love her, ye'll be proud she's got this here chance! Mebbe now Vinnie kin make somethin' o' herself!

CHORUS: A deceived, broken-hearted girl perhaps? Lutie, this villain is after her inheritance!

LUTIE: Now, Elmer, don't you go sayin' nothin' to Mr. Bascom. Ye jist be *noble* an' give Vinnie up. Jist let her *e*-lope an' I'll pertend I don't know nothin' about it. Now, I better get inside an' finish my chores. An' *you* better git on home, Elmer!

(LUTIE enters house, ELMER sits with head in hands. BEA-TRICE HUNTINGDON enters left.)

CHORUS: Uh-oh!

BEATRICE: Young man, has a man who calls himself Uttley Hunting-don been here?

ELMER: Huh?

BEATRICE: I said, has a man calling himself Uttley Huntingdon been here?

ELMER *(stands)*: Y-yes, ma'am!

BEATRICE: Oh, dear! I feared as much. Has he gone?

ELMER: No, ma'am. He's a-stayin' here until he can fix his autymobile. It's broke down.

BEATRICE: When will that be?

ELMER: It'll be fixed today.

BEATRICE *(looks around carefully)*: Tell me this: has he been up to *something* while he has been here?

ELMER: Well, uh—

BEATRICE *(dramatically)*: Oh, I have a right to ask, young man! Poor, unfortunate wretch that I am! For I am his neglected, deceived, and abused wife, Beatrice Huntingdon!

CHORUS: Ah-ha!

ELMER *(horrified)*: His *wife?* His wedded wife? Miz Huntingdon, he never said nothin' 'bout no wedded wife! Why, he's a-plannin' to *e*-lope with Vinnie Bascom tonight an' marry up with her over to the county seat!

43

BEATRICE: Just what I might have expected.

ELMER: But hit ain't legal! I mean if'n he's *yore* mate an' *yore* Miz Huntingdon, how kin Vinnie wed up with him, too, an' be Miz Huntingdon?

BEATRICE: Do you think bigamy would stop a man like Uttley?

CHORUS: *(Hiss.)*

BEATRICE: Is this girl wealthy?

ELMER: Wal, not 'zactly. 'Course the Bascoms has got a mighty tasty piece o' land here—an' Vinnie'll heir it all some day.

BEATRICE: The land! Of course. Uttley wants to get his greedy hands on the land.

CHORUS: Even if he has to take Vinnie with it temporarily.

ELMER: Pore Vinnie!

BEATRICE: Be grateful I arrived in time. This is the last straw. I have spent years pursuing Uttley, rescuing maidens in distress. Oh, I have had a miserable existence: bereft, betrayed by the man to whom I gave my heart, my hand, and my inheritance. Innocent girl that I was! *(Weeps. ELMER is acutely uncomfortable.)*

ELMER: I'm shore sorry to hear hit, Miz Huntingdon.

BEATRICE: Well, young man, I have rescued the last gullible female from Uttley's clutches! This time I will bring the sheriff here and we'll put Uttley behind bars.

ELMER: How's that, Miz Huntingdon?

BEATRICE: All we have to do is catch him as he starts out with that girl. Now, young man, not a word of this to any one! How can these girls fall for his line?

ELMER: Wal, now, he told the Bascoms he was a rich *in*-vestment broker.

BEATRICE: Investment broker indeed! He's never done an honest day's work in his life. He gambles or gets money from females with no sense and some money.

ELMER *(sadly):* Pore Vinnie.

BEATRICE: Poor Vinnie, indeed. She doesn't know how lucky she is.

CHORUS: How true. But she won't believe it.

BEATRICE: I'm going for the sheriff.

ELMER: Uh-huh.

BEATRICE: We'll meet you here tonight, over there. *(Points to "bush.")*

ELMER: Uh-huh.

BEATRICE *(dramatically to audience):* We will save this silly girl and defeat this dastardly villain!

(She leaves left. NEWT enters in time to see her.)

NEWT: Who was that there lady, Elmer? Whut did she want?

ELMER *(agitated):* Mr. Bascom! Mr. Bascom! You—you jist come right out to the barn! I gotta tell you something! Come on, Mr. Bascom!

(They go right. VINNIE tiptoes from house with suitcase and goes left. Lights dim to end scene.)

SCENE 4—that night

CHORUS: And so begins the last fatal scene of this tragedy. Will this innocent girl be led astray by the wiles of the villain? Will he succeed in his nefarious scheme? Or will a merciful fate intervene to rescue her? We shall see. We shall see.

(ELMER enters left, snoops around clumsily, then hides behind the "bush." BEATRICE enters, ELMER beckons and she too goes to the "bush.")

BEATRICE: Where is everyone?

ELMER: I reckon in the comp'ny parlor right now, a-talkin'. Hark ye! I shore hear someone comin'.

BEATRICE: I'll hide! *(She does but ELMER is still there when VINNIE appears at the door and sees him.)*

VINNIE *(coldly):* Is that you again, Elmer? I heerd woman-voice out here.

ELMER: Uh—I guess it wuz jist me a-talkin' to myself, I guess.

VINNIE: Elmer Wilkins, ye can be so silly! Or did ye come over fer somethin' special?

ELMER: I—Iwuz jist passin' by.

VINNIE: Wal, really, Elmer, there ain't no *from* to be going *to* by here, an' ye know hit! I'm shore ye'd be better off to home, stidda moonin' 'round here! So *good-night,* Elmer! *(She goes back in.)*

BEATRICE *(coming from concealment):* That young lady has dreadful manners.

ELMER: Oh, Vinnie's got *e-*lopin' on her mind an' she jist ain't herself.

BEATRICE: Whoever she is right now is certainly a rude person!

ELMER: I'd be proud to marry-up with Vinnie! But right now, she's bewitchēd.

BEATRICE: Uttley, no doubt. I cannot understand the power he holds over women.

ELMER: Oh, ma'am, he kin sure smooth-talk.

BEATRICE: Well, we had better talk. I am going for the sheriff now. I left him down the road a short distance. We will come back and hide over here. You'd better keep out of sight, too. When the time is right, we will confront the eloping lovers. I am sorry for your Vinnie, in a way, but this ought to make her appreciate you. You are a very nice boy, Elmer. Not too bright, but nice.

ELMER *(flattered):* Aw, thanks, Miz Huntingdon.

BEATRICE: I'll go now, Elmer.

(She leaves left. NEWT and LUTIE come from house.)

ELMER *(loud stage whisper):* Mr. Bascom! You an' Miz Bascom come over here!

LUTIE *(surprised):* What on earth ails ye, Elmer? Newt, whut's goin' on?

ELMER *(as they join him):* Wal, Miz Bascom, ye know Vinnie an' that Huntingdon feller is plannin' to *e-*lope tonight?

LUTIE: Aw, Elmer! Why're ye a blabber-mouth?

NEWT: I know hit all, Lutie.

46

ELMER: Miz Bascom, he's got a wife already! That Huntingdon feller—he has!

(LUTIE stifles a scream.) Yes, ma'am, he's a wedded man. An' he ain't no rich *in*-vestment broker like he tole you, but jist a—a gambler an' a no-good! (LUTIE moans.)

CHORUS: Your money, Lutie! He has your money!

ELMER: Miz Bascom, his pore wife is ri'cheer!

LUTIE (looking around, agitated): Here? Where at?

ELMER: Oh, she jist went down the road a piece to git the sheriff. Then they comin' back 'n' hide, to ketch that there Uttley when he goes to run off with Vinnie!

NEWT (sadly): I wischt there wuz a nother way. Pore Vinnie will be heart hurt. She'll be mighty lonely an' sad.

ELMER (sturdily): Wal, she's still got me, Mr. Bascom. Leastwise she kin have me.

CHORUS: Noble youth!

LUTIE (agitated): I jist gotta see that feller! He's got somethin'—I mean—well, I jist gotta, that's all! (She starts to house.)

NEWT (restraining her): Now, wait, Maw. Elmer, whut's your plan?

ELMER: Wal, me an' the sheriff an' Miz Huntingdon will hide over behind them bushes. You folks go to bed jist like always. Only don't really go to bed. Then when that there Uttley thinks yore asleep, him an' Vinnie'll e-lope. That's when the sheriff takes over.

LUTIE: O-o-oh, I don't think I can pertend.

NEWT: Yes, ye kin, 'cause hit's fer our little Vinnie. Vinnie's bin foolish like, but hit ain't rightly her fault, 'cause she don't know no better'n to be trustin'. Besides all them fancy promises sounded mighty likely to her—mighty likely.

LUTIE: Wal, if'n that's the way hit's got to be.

NEWT: Let's go in, Maw, and do whut we gotta do. See ye later, Elmer.

47

(They go inside, and ELMER to the "bush.")

CHORUS: So all is ready for the final outcome of this heartrending drama. The trap is set. There go the lights in the bedroom windows. Now, all wait for time to pass.

(BEATRICE and SHERIFF HIGGINS enter and hide behind "bush.")

SHERIFF: Howdy, Elmer. How's it goin'?
ELMER: Howdy, Sheriff Higgins! The Bascoms know everythin'. Their lights jist went out. Now we jist set an' wait.

BEATRICE: Listen! The door is opening!

(UTTLEY comes from house and stands listening. He strolls around looking satisfied.)

CHORUS *(softly):* Just you wait, Uttley! Little do you know what awaits you. Go ahead and look triumphant over the property you think you will get from that poor, simple girl. The wheels of justice are grinding, and soon all, even poor Vinnie, will know you for what you are, a villain, and a snake! *(Hiss.)*

(VINNIE comes from house. They clasp hands. He kisses hers extravagantly.)

UTTLEY: Ah, my moon flower! The time of waiting has seemed an infinity. My impatient eyes have hungered for the sight of your delectable charms.

CHORUS: It's her money showing.
VINNIE: Wal, I got tired a-waitin', too, Mr. Hunt—I mean, *Uttley.* Ever since I put my satchel in yore autymobile, hit's been plum time-draggin'.

UTTLEY: But now the time of waiting is over. Come, my dear, let us hasten away to joy and bliss forever! *(Puts arm around VINNIE and leads her to the right.)*

SHERIFF *(stepping from concealment):* Not so fast there, Mister! You be leavin', 'tis true, but not to joy an' bliss—an' not forever. Jist ten years, mebbe!

(UTTLEY and VINNIE stop in alarm. ELMER steps up beside SHERIFF.)

UTTLEY *(haughtily):* What is the meaning of this, sir?
VINNIE *(at same time):* Elmer! Ye here agin?

(The BASCOMS come from house and pull VINNIE away from UTTLEY.)

NEWT: We bin taken in, Vinnie. This here Uttley Huntingdon ain't no genteman a-tall. He's jist a crook! *(VINNIE is shocked.)*
LUTIE: Vinnie, baby, don't ye go grievin' yerself none fer sich a villain! Why he cain't wed you legal! He's got him a wedded wife already.

VINNIE *(weeping):* I cain't believe hit! I *don't* believe hit! Elmer, you done this. Ye jist made hit all up 'cause you wuz heart—jealous! *(She runs to UTTLEY, grabs his lapels desperately.)* Oh, Uttley, say this ain't true talk! All them purty words—Oh, say yore whut ye said ye wuz—an' ye ain't never bin wed a'tall!

BEATRICE *(dramatically, coming from concealment):* He *can't* say it, my dear, for *I* am his neglected, abandoned wife!

VINNIE *(moans and falls back against her father. ELMER goes to her side):* O-o-o-oh!

UTTLEY *(furiously):* Beatrice! What are you doing here? I thought you were safely in New York! This is all your doing! I should have killed you long ago!

(He lunges at her. The SHERIFF stops him forcibly and puts on handcuffs in the struggle.)

SHERIFF: You ain't killin' nobody! An' mebbe when ye git outa state's prison, ye'll be too tired an' old to go 'round villain'in an' makin' yore pore wife traipse after ye! Come on! I'm takin' ye to jail!

(SHERIFF takes UTTLEY off left but not before LUTIE darts to UTTLEY'S side and retrieves her money from his pocket. NEWT watches her amazed.)

BEATRICE *(to Vinnie):* My dear, you are young. You will recover from this unfortunate love affair. It wasn't real love at all, it was just a fascination. You will realize this soon. You have a young man right here who truly loves you deeply. I refer to Elmer Wilkins. I will go now, but I hope to hear soon that you are Mrs. Elmer Wilkins!

(She leaves left. They watch her go then look at VINNIE, who goes to ELMER.)

VINNIE: Oh, Elmer! Kin ye ever forgive me? I bin so silly!
CHORUS: Go on, Elmer, forgive her. You might as well. It's in the plot!
ELMER: Shore, Vinnie. Ye wuz jist bewitched by that there slick Uttley. Wal, ye can still have me! Anyways, time we git married-up and have five or six younguns, ye won't remember that ol' Uttley any more. *(He takes her in the house.)*

CHORUS: She won't have time.
NEWT: Wal, 'pears like things is turnin' out fer the best after all. Say, Lutie, jist whut did ye take from that feller's pocket?

LUTIE: I ain't gonna tell ye!
NEWT *(warning):* Lutie! Ain't ye done enough? 'Twarn't all Vinnie, ye know.

LUTIE: Wal, all right. I bin savin' near five years jest to git some bridal pretties fer Vinnie when she weds. I give hit to that Uttley to *invest.* He promised I'd git hit an' more back in no time!

NEWT: I reckon ye better let me take keer o' hit.
LUTIE: Now, Newt, ye don't want that there money!

50

NEWT: Yes, I do, too, Lutie. Vinnie don't need so many fancy fixins'. After all, she's jist gonna wed Elmer. They gonna need somethin' 'sides fancy fixin's. I cal'clate I'll git a new plow for Elmer with that there money. 'Pears like that boy's got more sense 'n' any of us.

(They enter house.)

CHORUS: So our friend Elmer gets not only Vinnie, without fancy fixings, but a shiny new plow to make his noble heart glad. Thus ends our gripping story. The dastardly villain was outwitted. True love triumphed. Long live Elmer and Vinnie! May their tribe increase!

THE END

CASE FOR SAMARIA

This fun drama makes no pretensions to truth other than the facts of the original story of the Good Samaritan found in Luke 10:30-35. It preaches no doctrine; it intends no sacrilege. Among the reasons for which God made laughter, one must be that man might not take himself too seriously.

This is comedy and should be played for laughs. Comedy is a matter of timing, of unusual inflections, of unexpected bits of stage "business," of exaggerated acting, and the right costumes and make-up.

TIME: Twenty years after the story of the Good Samaritan in Luke 10.

PLACE: A bedroom in the palace of the High Priest, the Priest of the original story. In stage center, extending downstage is a couch with pillows and rich covering. A stool at the right of the bed, two more at stage left back, and a bench downstage far right complete the necessary furniture. Other accessories such as rugs or urns, could be added. Necessary exits right and left. Focus all lighting on the couch area, leaving exits in semi-obscurity.

SITUATION: As the play opens, the High Priest is lying upon the couch waiting for death. Or, rather, the Heavenly Messenger who is coming to escort him to his just reward. His friend of many years, the Levite of the original story, is seated on the stool at the right of the couch.

CAST (in order of appearance)

Note: All costumes are vaguely biblical.

HIGH PRIEST—about sixty years old, ensconced in state on the couch. Sumptiously overdressed, with all the panoply of his office for this occasion of his departure to the other world. He overacts always.

LEVITE—also about sixty. Costume exaggerated, especially the hat.

UBO—an angel of death, the Heavenly Messenger. Unlike any imagined angel: scrawny, undersized, in a clean but worn and patched robe. His ill-fitting halo is tarnished and askew. He wears a shoulder bag or satchel in which to carry his "list." His expression is doleful, his voice high and whining. He has a bad case of the sniffles.

LETHA—the Priest's wife, a plain woman around fifty, well-dressed in a fussy way. Talks constantly, is over-emotional and not too intelligent.

MARUM and BEIRA—the Priest's two homely daughters, middle-aged and over-dressed.

AZRA—an angel of higher rank, tall, fine looking, well robed, a scarf draped across his head.

MAN—the original victim on the Jericho road, dead these last ten years.

THE SAMARITAN—original rescuer of the MAN, dead now six years. Dress MAN and SAMARITAN in over all covering with only faces showing. Match clothing to background for obscurity. Make faces to look white and unreal, yet human.

THE INNKEEPER—about forty-five, strong looking, dressed as to his station in life.

53

LEVITE *(grieving nobly):* It will not be long now until the Heavenly Messenger comes for you!

PRIEST *(also in lofty drama):* I am ready, old friend! I am ready.

LEVITE *(over-emotional):* I shall miss you.

PRIEST: Ah, yes. Among the good things I've had in my lifetime—power, wealth, position—none has been more satisfying than your long friendship.

LEVITE: Remembering that, old friend, I shall face my own *going* with fortitude. *(Piously aside to heaven.)* May it be distant!

PRIEST *(sighs):* Yes.

LEVITE *(eloquently): There* you will be for blissful eternity, leaving all earthly problems behind you!

PRIEST *(sighs gustily):* Yes!

LEVITE *(even more eloquently):* Surrounded by heavenly beauty, taking none of the crass things of the world with you!

PRIEST *(looking around, doubtfully):* Ye-es.

LEVITE: Ah, my dear, dear, *dear* old friend! Thinking of the realm you are about to enter, I envy you! I positively *envy* you!

PRIEST *(a trifle acidly):* Well, let's not get carried away! I can think of reasons for staying around a while longer!

LEVITE: Your affairs are in order aren't they?

PRIEST: Naturally! Of course, there will be the problem of selecting my successor, the new High Priest. The choice lies between Arum and Belioz. You know how they feel toward each other. That will be some fight! I wish I could be here to see it. It's a long time ago now, but I well remember the things *I* did to win out over Bildad. *(Piously.)* May his soul rest in peace!

LEVITE *(reminding him):* You will be seeing Bildad. Soon.

PRIEST *(uncomfortable):* No! Yes, I guess you're right. Well, maybe there he will have forgotten.

LEVITE: I doubt that Bildad has changed that much. Now what about your family?

PRIEST: My nephew, Ephrem, will look after my wife and daughters.

LEVITE: Isn't he the nephew who tried to make something of that miserable Tekoan Wilderness property and failed disastrously?

PRIEST *(with relish):* Yes, poor fellow! I feel sorry for him, but not enough to let him out of our bargain.

LEVITE: Bargain?

PRIEST: Yes. I paid his debts and gave him the income from the Judean olive groves for life. In return he is to take care of my wife and daughters until they die, or marry. *(Grins diabolically.)* And he was so-o-o grateful, poor fellow!

LEVITE: Poor fellow! His guardianship will last a long, long time.

PRIEST: *Years!* Letha is as healthy as a horse. I can just picture his life with that woman around. She looks upon silence as a personal enemy and what a fight she puts up!

LEVITE: Your daughters—

PRIEST: Poor homely creatures! *(Sighs.)* They take after their mother, of course.

LEVITE: You married her.

PRIEST: Well I was involved in a little transaction. Oh, nothing illegal, you understand, but it was better kept quiet. Letha's father found out about it. Well, he *did* give the Judean olive lands as a marriage portion. I wasn't rich then.

LEVITE: Surely such a clever man as you could have found someone to marry your daughters, Beira and Marum?

PRIEST: Do you think I would stoop to blackmail? *(LEVITE nods vigorously.)* Well, I did offer very handsome doweries. But there wasn't any way I could manage to keep the young men from *seeing* those girls before the ceremony!

LEVITE *(consoling):* They can always fill their lives with good works. Don't let it worry—

(He breaks off abruptly as UBO enters left. The two look at him in amazement.)

LEVITE: Who—who are you?

UBO *(sniffs, nasally whining voice):* The Heavenly Messenger you've been expecting.

BOTH: Oh, no!

UBO *(defensively):* Well, I *am* an angel. Ubo, I'm called. Ubo, the Heavenly Messenger! *(Sniff.)*

PRIEST *(aghast):* There must be some mistake!

UBO *(plaintively):* That's what all my—*clients*—say. They are always disappointed. Come, now. I'm in a hurry. This is the rush season. The fighting, you know. Are you ready? *(Nears the couch.)*

LEVITE *(agitated):* My friend, stop! You have to think of appearances! You can't go with him!

PRIEST *(indignantly):* Of course not! I can just hear the tongues clacking all over Jerusalem. I think there's been a mistake!

UBO *(sniffs):* We don't make mistakes.

PRIEST: This isn't personal. Don't feel hurt.

UBO: Angels can't afford that extravagance.

PRIEST: I—I know I have to go. But it is fitting that I leave with someone who looks more—*angelic,* if you know what I mean.

UBO *(sighs):* I do. But you're on my *list. (Pats his satchel.)* So you'd better come along. *(Reaches for him.)*

PRIEST *(scrambles out of reach):* Weren't there any more-qualified angels available?

UBO: Oh, I'm qualified, all right. Would you like the testimonials of some of those I've conducted?

PRIEST: No! No, that's all right! I'm sure you do a good job.

UBO: Then let's go.

PRIEST *(stubbornly):* I am the High Priest! I *can't* go with *you!*

UBO *(removes halo, scratches his head and puts halo back on, crooked):* This resistance hasn't come up in other cases. *(Sniff.)* I don't know what to do.

LEVITE *(helpfully):* Isn't there someone you can report to? Someone higher up, maybe, who can do something about this?

UBO: Well, there's Azra.

LEVITE: Is he an angel higher up?

UBO: Yes, he's the Supervisor of the Heavenly Messengers of the Israel District.

LEVITE: Then get him!

UBO *(sighs):* You won't change your mind?

PRIEST: No!

UBO: I'll go get him, then. *(Turns away slowly.)*

PRIEST *(impatiently):* And you might hurry! I haven't got all day, you know! *(Ubo shrugs, leaves left.)* Someone has made a mistake. You'd think *they'd* run things better. *(Outside loud wailing is heard.)* What is all that caterwauling?

LEVITE *(jumps up, shouting above noise, as PRIEST'S wife and daughters enter. Wife is wailing loudly and daughters are noisily comforting her):* It's your wife and daughters!

PRIEST: Don't shout! I can see! Oh, shut up, woman! Why are you making such a racket?

LETHA *(emotionally throwing herself across the couch and grasping him by the knees. Her sentences merge rapidly):* Oh, my precious husband, father of my children, how can we face life without you? Our darling girls, no father! My heart is breaking, when I think how often I've known I'd be the first to go since I'm so delicate! Did you ever think when we gave our vows—little did I believe this day would ever—

PRIEST *(as LEVITE tries to pull her off, he shouts but makes no impression on her flow of speech):* Quiet, woman! Quiet!

LETHA: —come and would I be left to mourn and remember the years we had. Don't you remember the day? Did you ever think you would be the one? Oh, my poor, poor husband, I shall always cherish your memory and will keep your name before your poor little grandchildren, if you ever have any, and they will—

PRIEST *(places his hand over her mouth):* What do you want?
LETHA *(as he temporarily removes hand):* We have come to anoint you for death! *(Hand again.)*

MARUM and BEIRA: For death, father. *(Beira shows him a vial of oil.)*
PRIEST: Well, you needn't sound so cheerful about it! Get out of here, both of you, and take your mother with you. I'm busy. *(Removes hand.)*

LETHA *(wailing, as the LEVITE pulls her up):* But it is the custom! Every good wife and daughter helps to anoint the men of the household for death! You can't deny us the right to perform this last token of love we have for you. Customs can't be tossed aside. Everybody expects—

PRIEST *(shouts so loud Letha shuts up):* A *barbarous* custom! A man is down and uncomfortable already. And then you want to pour cold, clammy, messy oil all over his defenseless head? I won't have it!

MARUM *(whining):* It is our right, Father!
BEIRA: What will our friends say?
PRIEST: Plenty, probably, but I won't be around to hear it.
LETHA *(tries to throw self on couch but Levite holds her back):* O-o-oh, hu-usband!

PRIEST *(shouts):* Out! Out!! *(To Levite.)* Get them out of here! *(He tries.)* When I'm ready to die, I'll tell you. Oh, I'll let you hold up your heads in public at the expense of your poor, unfortunate father! Right now I'm busy. Letha, go away. Take those, those *girls* with you. The least they could have done for their father before he dies was to get husbands!

BEIRA *(wailing):* Oh, father, how can you reproach us!

PRIEST: Has any father done more to bring about marriages for his daughters? And I almost succeeded. What about that young vintner from Lebanon? He actually was ready to negotiate for you, Marum. And what did you do?

MARUM: N-nothing, father!

PRIEST: That's just it! Nothing! What kind of wife did he think you'd make, standing there with your mouth open every time he spoke to you, and not a word in reply?

MARUM: But Mother said a husband wants a wife who will be silent!

PRIEST: Too bad *her* mother didn't teach *her* that!

BEIRA *(puts arm around weeping mother):* Father, you aren't being fair!

PRIEST: Fair? Well, what about you? Did you take advantage of the fine marriage I almost arranged for you? He was a silk merchant—*silk,* mind you! Why, you could have been a rich woman.

BEIRA: He was *fat!* And besides he had buried two wives already. And—and he *belched!*

PRIEST: Do you consider yourself a delicate morsel who could be swallowed without making a man belch?

BEIRA *(wailing):* Father, you are cruel!

(The women weep loudly. The PRIEST pretends to feel faint, groans dramatically, and sinks down limply on the pillows.)

LEVITE *(hastily):* This isn't good for him! You'd better go quickly. *(Pushes them toward exit.)*

LETHA *(alarmed):* Oh, my! Come, girls, at once. *(To LEVITE.)* Oh, *do* something for him! Can I help?

LEVITE: No, no. I can look after him. I'll call you if you are needed. *(Succeeds in pushing them out. Returns to Priest.)*

PRIEST *(feebly):* Have—have they gone?
LEVITE: Yes.
PRIEST *(heartily, sitting up):* Good riddance! They'll be the death of me yet.

(UBO enters with AZRA. The men are visibly impressed.)

UBO: Well, here's Azra. *(Sniff.)*
LEVITE *(nervously backing away):* It—it is my friend here, who is to—*go.*

AZRA *(walks slowly down front left and turns majestically. Rich, deep voice):* I know. *(To PRIEST.)* He tells me you refuse to go with him.

PRIEST: Yes!
AZRA: Why?
PRIEST: Do you know I am the High Priest?
AZRA: We know.
PRIEST: Then you know what people would think if it ever got out that *he* was sent to take me! Just look at him! I won't go!

UBO *(plucks AZRA'S sleeve):* What did I tell you? *(Sniff.)*
AZRA: Actually you have no choice. According to the time schedule, you are overdue already. But, in your case, heaven's mercy has been extended. We shall try to make our ways clear to you.

LEVITE: My friend only wants you to do the proper thing.
AZRA: The proper thing here is not always acceptable there. On earth, there are differences in station, wealth, advantages, privileges and the like. In heaven, if you make it, you will find differences of reward for life here.

LEVITE: But he is *High Priest* and rates the *best!*
AZRA: On earth, perhaps. But according to our record *(Consults papers or a ledger.)* You rate a Class C angel and Class C dwelling place beyond. Ubo, here, is a Class C angel.

Ubo *(proudly):* I sure am!

Priest *(viewing Ubo distastefully):* Then *what* is a Class C dwelling?

Azra: Material things matter little there. However, a Class C dwelling is a one room cabin with a door and two windows.

Levite *(amazed):* No solarium? No upper room? My friend has always had the best! Look about you. Why he couldn't *live* in one room!

Azra: Then that's no problem.

Levite: What do you mean, no problem?

Azra: He won't be alive. *(Ubo sniffs loudly.)*

> *(LETHA appears at right entrance, talking over her shoulder to her daughters, close behind her. They aren't aware of the newcomers in the room.)*

Letha: And so we cannot put it off any longer. It isn't seemly. He must be made to see that. He has always been so careful of what people thought. A little thing like dying couldn't alter his feelings that much. He must let us— *(She breaks off as she sees the angels and stifles a scream. Daughters are alarmed.)* Who—who are *they?*

Priest *(crossly):* Who do you think they are? Egyptian mummies? Letha, leave this room until I send for you. We are *in conference.*

Letha: You mean—they are—Oh, no! *(She faints, sinking to floor.)*

Marum *(kneeling and wailing, rubbing mother's hands and patting her cheeks):* Oh, mother! Oh, mother, not you, too! Not you, too!

Ubo: Unfortunately, no. She's not on my list.

Beira: Don't be silly, Marum. She's just fainted.

Levite: She might come to! *(He either picks her up and carries her off right or drags her off, depending on sizes. Daughters follow.)*

Priest: Women! Are there women—*there?* *(AZRA nods.)* Ugh! *(Shudder.)*

61

LEVITE *(returns, puffing):* I left her on the floor out there. She's heavy.

UBO: Azra, I'd better get on with this. There's another client waiting for me.

AZRA: Are you ready to go with Ubo?

PRIEST *(looking at Ubo in distaste):* Don't you have any better looking messengers? Surely, all messengers aren't like Ubo?

AZRA: Indeed no. Some angels are magnificent, and some dwellings mansions, even more beautiful than this.

LEVITE *(indignantly, going down right):* Then why is the High Priest subjected to such indignity? Who decides such things? How is it decided?

AZRA: We are wasting time, borrowed time. Go with Ubo! *(UBO turns to leave.)*

UBO: I'm one behind now.

PRIEST *(sits up):* Wait! Didn't you promise that heaven's mercy has been extended and you would make things clear to me before I—went?

UBO *(sniffs sadly):* That's what he said.

AZRA: I did, didn't I? Very well then. The Highest decides. Your life's record determines the decision.

LEVITE: But he is *High Priest!* Do you know how much is necessary for a man to reach that station?

UBO: Yes, and he did it all!

PRIEST: I stack my record against anyone's!

AZRA *(at stage front):* I have your record here. *(Looks through papers or ledger.)* Let's see. Here's something cancelled. And here cancelled. Oh, here's one, a very black mark—*uncancelled!*

PRIEST: For what?

AZRA: The incident of the man on the road between Jericho and Jerusalem.

PRIEST *(bewildered):* What man?

AZRA: The man you saw stripped and wounded unto death, and passed on by twenty years ago.

PRIEST *(indignantly):* Stripped and wou— That's ridiculous! I don't know what you're talking about!

LEVITE: You mean you would hold something against a man for twenty years? That's so long ago!

AZRA: Years mean nothing to us. Yesterday is today is tomorrow. Time does not erase your record. It merely adds to it, one way or the other.

LEVITE: Do you mean a man can't live down his past?

AZRA: Quite the contrary. But the passing of years means nothing. To make a man's past useful to him, we provide two elements: memory and conscience. When he uses these elements, and makes restitution in kind and in spirit, his past is not counted against him. But, in this case, neither safeguard was used.

LEVITE *(arguing):* But you heard him say he doesn't remember it!

AZRA: Men forget many things they choose not to remember. And you? I see here you were also present that day.

LEVITE: No! I don't remember it either. It couldn't amount to much if neither of us remembers it.

AZRA: To the man, it meant his life.

PRIEST: Sounds fishy to me. Just who was this man?

AZRA: A countryman of yours travelling that road.

UBO *(goes right):* A well travelled road. *Accidents* happen there. I'm there often on business. *(Sniffs.)*

AZRA *(approaching Priest):* This was no accident. This Hebrew had been beaten unmercifully, stabbed several times, stripped of his clothing and possessions, and cast by the side of the road to die. *You* came that way, observed him there across the road and didn't even stop to see if you could help him.

PRIEST: I still don't remember it. *(To Levite.)* Do you?

LEVITE *(going behind head of couch):* No. Perhaps I didn't see him.

AZRA: Oh, yes, you saw him. In fact, you crossed the road and looked more closely. Then went your way.

PRIEST: Surely I would remember. *(Suspiciously.)* How do you know this is true? Perhaps an error has been made in my record?

UBO *(sniffs): We* don't make mistakes.
LEVITE: Everyone else does!
UBO: We're different.
LEVITE *(glaring at him):* Obviously.
PRIEST: Someone could have made up this story.
AZRA: Oh, man, you strain heaven's mercy! But you shall have opportunity yet to know why judgment was passed.

LEVITE *(to Priest):* How can we be sure he is telling the truth? How do we know these two are even—*messengers?* They *could* be—

AZRA *(sternly):* Be careful, Levite! If you want to live out your allotted span!

UBO: Can I add him to my list, Azra?
LEVITE: No offense meant! I just wanted to be sure.
AZRA: Heaven's mercy seems wasted on you. But we'll try again. Would you believe the testimony of the man who was so grievously wounded?

LEVITE: Unless he is being paid by our enemies to tell such a tale.
AZRA: Where he is, money means nothing. I hardly think even your enemies are strong enough to reach from beyond the grave.

LEVITE *(nervously):* He *died* on the road?
AZRA: No, he recovered.
PRIEST: Then why all the fuss?
AZRA: His wounds were so severe that he would have died had not another given the aid you denied.

LEVITE: Then someone did stop to help him?
AZRA: Yes, a Samaritan.
LEVITE: I'll never believe anything good of a Samaritan! *(Plunks down on the stool by the couch.)*

PRIEST *(agreeing):* The only good Samaritan is a dead one.

AZRA: Then you will heartily approve of this one. He *is* dead. Ubo, summon the men, both of them.

UBO *(plaintively):* All right. *(He goes left center, back to audience, hands over eyes, deep concentration. Suddenly two figures appear before him. If their costumes are the same color as the background and the lighting is dim at the left entrance, they can slip in during the preceding lines and simply turn around to become visible. PRIEST and LEVITE give startled exclamations and LEVITE jumps to his feet. LETHA and daughters step into right entrance at same time and muffle screams. PRIEST hears them.)*

PRIEST: I told you to stay out!

LETHA *(at couch):* Please let us come in! I won't say a word. No matter what happens, I won't say one word, even if I do think a wife should have something to say when her husband is—oh—*(She shuts up quickly at his threatening gesture.)*

MARUM *(daughters try to lead Letha away):* She really won't, Father. And we won't try to anoint you.

BEIRA: And Mother won't faint again, will you, Mother?

LETHA: No. And I shall restrain my tears, although when I think how sad—*(Beira covers her mother's mouth with her hand.)*

PRIEST: Very well. Sit over there and be quiet. *(Indicates bench.)* Remember: *no interruptions!*

LETHA: No,—I—*(Beira covers her mouth again and leads her to bench.)*

MARUM: We promise.

BEIRA: Not a word. *(The three sit.)*

PRIEST *(looking at them):* And to think I have to die to see this!

UBO *(leading two dead men to group):* Here they are. This is the man who was left to die by the side of the road. *(Sniff.)* And this is the Samaritan. *(Sniff.)*

LEVITE *(jumps up and stands dramatically between newcomers and the women):* Make him stand in plain sight! The Samaritan, I mean. I don't trust him!

UBO: But he's dead. They both are. They can't hurt you.

LEVITE: Dead or not, I don't trust a Samaritan!

PRIEST *(shouting):* Letha, Marum, Beira! Stay over there! *(The women jump to their feet and huddle in alarm.)*

UBO *(also jumps):* Don't *do* that! You scared me. What's the matter?

PRIEST: He's a *Samaritan!*

MARUM: Oh, Father, save us!

BEIRA: Don't let him get us, Father!

LETHA: Oh, save our innocent girls! Save our babies!

UBO *(unbelieving):* You think—*those women* are in danger?

PRIEST: All Samaritans are low-born, despoilers of women, thieves, liars, cheats!

UBO *(sniffs):* Anything else?

LEVITE: Surely, even over *there* you have heard about Samaritans?

UBO: Of course. We have quite a few of them.

LEVITE: No! What is the world coming to!

UBO: The *world* isn't, unfortunately. *(Sniff.)*

AZRA *(walks slowly right front):* In any event you have nothing to fear from this one. He has been what you call dead for ten years. *(The women sit again.)*

PRIEST: His presence, dead or alive, is unwelcome here! I won't lower myself by associating with a Samaritan.

UBO: What a surprise you've got coming.

AZRA: According to the record, he came out far better than you did.

LEVITE *(follows Azra):* No Samaritan is the equal of a Hebrew!

AZRA: He did what you should have done: rescued your country-man, saved his life.

UBO: *I* wasn't working this district then.

LEVITE: We can question them? Then we want them where we can keep our eyes on them! *(Brings two stools from backstage to left of couch as he talks.)* They can sit here where we can see them. They can *sit,* can't they?

AZRA: Oh, yes. They retain many of the properties of life, but none of the necessities.

PRIEST *(interested):* Is that so? That's interesting. I'd like to know more about this.

UBO: You will. First hand. Soon, I hope. *(Stands behind couch.)*

LEVITE *(backs away as SAMARITAN and MAN sit on stools):* Now, we can watch you! *(Assumes over-drawn attitude of prosecuting attorney.)* You! This—angel—says you were beaten and robbed and left for dead on the road between Jericho and Jerusalem. Is this statement true?

MAN: Yes, it's true. Happened about ten years before I died.

LEVITE: What were you doing there? Looking for trouble?

MAN: My business took me along that road. I was a travelling merchant.

PRIEST *(slyly):* Hmmm. Perhaps you made enemies.

MAN: *Our* common enemies: Roman soldiers.

LEVITE: Romans? Heaven preserve us!

AZRA: It will. Eventually.

PRIEST: Roman patrols regularly appear on that road. I've seen them many times. None ever attacked me.

MAN *(sadly):* Perhaps you never met a group far gone in wine and spoiling for trouble. I did. They made me get off my beast, demanded my money. I tried to reason with them. This only made them angry. One of them struck me and I resisted. Then we were all fighting. Then I remember nothing.

LEVITE *(pacing in front of MAN):* Ah, ha! That's a point! You remember nothing? Not us? Not the Samaritan? *(He shakes his head. LEVITE triumphantly to group.)* He remembers nothing!

MAN: Not for a while, at least. When I came to myself again, I was in that roadside inn, very weak, barely alive. I had several stab wounds and my head had been badly beaten.

PRIEST: The important thing is that you were still alive.

MAN: No thanks to those who saw me and did nothing!

PRIEST: Perhaps there were extenuating circumstances.

MAN: Well, I nearly *died* of those extenuating circumstances! If it hadn't been for that Samaritan—

PRIEST: Samaritan! And you a Hebrew!

MAN: Flowing blood does not ask the name of the one that staunches it! Yes, the Samaritan stopped. He didn't ask if I were a Samaritan too, before he dressed my wounds! Then he covered my nakedness with his own cloak, put me on his beast and took me to that inn. Wait! That wasn't all. He paid for my care there. Remember I had no money. He even arranged with the innkeeper to pay later if there were additional cost.

PRIEST: And demanded payment from you, over and over, a hundredfold, no doubt! One of the worst fates that can befall a Hebrew is to find himself in the financial clutches of an unscrupulous Samaritan!

MAN: You are wrong. For the ten years I lived I tried to find him to repay my debt.

LEVITE *(triumphantly):* Ah, ha! Another point. Where was he hiding?

MAN: The innkeeper didn't know his name or city. He had always known him as "the Samaritan."

LEVITE: How do you know your rescuer *was* a Samaritan?

MAN: The innkeeper told me.

LEVITE *(dramatically):* Told you? *Told* you? Hearsay evidence! Entirely inadmissable! For all you know, your rescuer could have been an Egyptian or a Numidian! Answer truthfully.

MAN: We-e-ell. Yes, I suppose so. I had no reason to doubt the word of the innkeeper.

LEVITE: Do you go around trusting everybody?

UBO: That will be the day!

MAN: I trusted the innkeeper. He was a Hebrew and had no particular love for Samaritans.

AZRA: A sad reason. Built on mutual hate.

MAN: Then later, the Samaritan told me himself.

LEVITE: What do you mean, later? I thought you couldn't find him?

MAN: I couldn't. Alive, that is. But, since then—

LEVITE: Oh. You mean?

MAN: Yes.

LEVITE: Hmmm. *(To Samaritan with a shudder.)* You! I find it hard to speak civilly to a Samaritan, even a dead one. This is the story you told the innkeeper and this man?

SAMARITAN: Yes. When I saw him that day, I thought he was dead and almost passed on by.

LEVITE *(to AZRA):* See there? Even he thought the man was dead!

SAMARITAN: But I stopped to make sure.

PRIEST *(sarcastically):* Perhaps you thought there was something the thieves might have overlooked.

SAMARITAN: Even I could see that the man had nothing, either around him or on him! A naked Hebrew looks much the same as a naked Samaritan.

LETHA *(intrigued):* Oh, is that so? Did you hear that, girls? I've always heard that Samaritans have great purple circles on their backs—as a mark! Tell me—

MARUM *(excited):* Do Samaritans have six toes? I've heard that, lots of times.

BEIRA: Oh, Marum, that isn't what you heard! You always get things mixed up. It's the people south of Egypt that have six toes. Samaritans have little forked tails.

SAMARITAN: I'm sorry to disillusion you. We are quite indistinguishable from other men. No, *I* was always told there was a mysterious extra arm coming from a Hebrew's side, which he covered with his robe. *(The women utter protests.)* No, I found out that was wrong. The man by the roadside proved that.

PRIEST: Marum! Beira! Do you want me to put you out again?

MARUM: No, Father.

LEVITE: Now, then. Are you sure you didn't make this all up? You didn't, for instance, come along this road and see this man in a dazed condition? You didn't investigate and see some few things the robbers overlooked? And then you didn't inflict greater wounds and take everything for yourself? And finally, you didn't cover your crime by this wild tale to a gullible inn-keeper?

SAMARITAN: No. Why should I do these things?

UBO: Yes, why would he do these things?

LEVITE: Because he's a Samaritan. Have you forgotten that Samaritans are notorious liars, thieves, torturers, libertines?

UBO: How could we forget with you reminding us?

PRIEST: Aren't we losing sight of the main issue? My part in this so-called crime?

AZRA: Indeed, we have not lost sight of it.

PRIEST: If this man was unconscious, how does he know it was *I* who passed him by?

AZRA: He doesn't know. We do.

PRIEST: You have witnesses who saw me?

AZRA: We need no human witnesses. We have our ways. It is all here in your record.

LETHA *(goes to husband):* My husband is a good, kind, thoughtful man! *(Begins to weep.)* He would never—he would *never* pass up a fellow creature in such distress! I—I know he wouldn't! Why—why, he *couldn't!*

MARUM *(aside to Beira):* I'm not so sure.

BEIRA: Nor I. Marum, do you remember the time—

MARUM: Sh!

PRIEST *(patting LETHA'S hand):* There, there. Thank you, my dear. A very discerning, intelligent woman. *(To LEVITE.)* I've often said so, haven't I, old friend?

LEVITE: Oh, indeed. Your very words: "a discerning, intelligent woman."

AZRA: Your record does not lie. It shows you did pass the man by.

LEVITE: You say so. But why would my noble friend do such a thing?

AZRA: According to this, he had a business appointment and was in a hurry.

LEVITE: Since when has it become a sin to be punctual?

AZRA: An overworked virtue can be more vicious than sin.

UBO: Sin or virtue, I wish he'd make up his mind. I'm *two* behind schedule now. *(Sniffs and sits sadly against left wall.)*

AZRA: Then he said to himself, "Oh, the man is probably dead already." But he didn't go to see.

LEVITE: Wait a minute! How do you know what he said to himself?

AZRA: We know all his thoughts. We know what you are thinking now.

LEVITE *(uncomfortably):* Oh.

PRIEST: If *I* think a man looks dead, he's *dead.*

UBO: But he isn't. I mean, he is, too. I mean he is now, but he wasn't then.

LETHA *(to UBO):* Dead or not, what does it matter to you? Anybody who's here to—take my poor husband—O-ooh—*(Weeps.)*

AZRA: Heaven provides death as a climax to life, the promise of fulfillment. But life is death's proving ground and all men must be perfected.

MARUM: Well, I think you are too hard on our poor, dying father. He just made a little old mistake in judgment!

BEIRA: Be quiet, Marum. Our father does not make mistakes. He's said so, often enough.

LETHA: But girls, don't you remember the time—?

PRIEST: Letha!

AZRA: Well, he made a mistake this time, for the man was not dead.

LEVITE: It has not been proved to our satisfaction that the whole story isn't fiction!

UBO *(to himself):* I wonder when *he* comes up on my list?

71

AZRA *(sternly):* You blind yourself willfully! What do you think of this, then? He thought, "Here is a badly wounded man. Why, he has nothing, not even clothing. Oh, well, just another beggar. Palestine is full of destitute beggars. What is one beggar, more or less? He won't be missed." Then he went on his way.

LEVITE: He was right! Palestine *is* full of beggars. It is all the fault of these Romans.

AZRA: Don't you feel any responsibility for them? These unfortunates are your countrymen.

LEVITE: Why my responsibility? The Romans are in charge of the country. Let the Romans worry about them. Not that they will, of course. Romans have no pity, no mercy. Their cruelty is well known. Why, for *pleasure,* they watch men kill each other in the arena. Thousands gather to watch and enjoy it!

PRIEST: Don't forget our cities are filled with the destitute. Many of them die by the roadside and on city streets.

UBO: I know. How well I know! As of five minutes ago, I am four behind schedule.

AZRA: You gave yourself a fourth "reason." You could see his wounds, even across the road. You didn't want to be involved in a murder case.

PRIEST: Well! One can't be involved in murder, even innocently, without having someone point the finger of suspicion. I decided twenty years ago to become High Priest. My reputation meant a lot to me.

AZRA: And so, because of fear of what someone might say you would condemn a man to death?

LEVITE: I object to that statement! He didn't try to kill the man!
AZRA: Death by inaction is just as fatal for the victim as death by intent.

72

UBO: Yes, I just take them as they come.

LEVITE: What would *you* call sufficient reasons?

AZRA: To abandon a man to death? You are thinking your reasons might have been sufficient?

LEVITE: Well—yes. If I was ever there.

AZRA: You were. And you will be judged for it. *(Looks at ledger.)* You did walk across the road and you did look down at the man. You thought, "Oh, well, he can't live long anyway. I must hurry to catch up with my friend." And you left.

LEVITE *(defensively):* We always had a lot of business together.

UBO *(sniff):* I can imagine some of it.

AZRA: Then you thought, "How repulsive. The sight of blood always makes me feel ill. It isn't good for me to stay here."

LEVITE: If the sight of blood makes one feel ill, it's no sin to get away!

UBO: Why not tell the army that?

AZRA: Finally, you justified yourself by thinking, "Someone will come along and help him. There's no need for me to become involved."

LEVITE *(triumphantly):* I was right! Someone did.

MAN: Yes, this Samaritan.

LEVITE: No good Samaritan!

AZRA: How many Samaritans have you known personally?

LEVITE: None! If you think I would associate with a Samaritan—

AZRA: Isn't that condemning a whole people without any personal knowledge of guilt?

LEVITE: Not when they're Samaritans!

UBO *(sniff):* I'm glad I'm not human. It's bad enough to be *five* behind schedule.

AZRA: *(goes to PRIEST):* After all you've heard, do you still question the judgment upon you?

PRIEST: I still can't remember. I will not accept this as final proof.

LEVITE: Surely you can do better than you have. You angels are sup-

73

posed to have quite a bit of power, aren't you?

UBO *(sniff):* Go on and show him, Azra!

AZRA: *(to center front, over the audience):* O, ye with hearts of stone! But we shall do all we can. *(To others.)* Would you accept the testimony of the innkeeper? He *is* one of your countrymen.

PRIEST: Then we will listen to what he has to say.

UBO *(dismayed):* But Azra, he isn't dead yet! He's never been on my list.

MARUM *(moves toward others):* Not dead? Oh, is he young?

BEIRA *(following her):* What's more important, is he married?

LETHA *(following, reproving):* Now, girls, this is no time to be thinking of — *(Stops.)* Although, come to think of it, it's foolish to pass up an opportunity. Dear, would it be wrong for our girls to marry an innkeeper? Just one of them, of course. Would she be looked down on socially, and what about—

PRIEST: Letha!

LETHA: Oh!

UBO: Azra, didn't you hear me? He isn't dead yet!

AZRA: I know.

UBO: How can I bring him if he isn't dead?

AZRA: We knew what they would think and that this was going to happen.

PRIEST: How could you know what we would think?

LEVITE: We didn't know ourselves.

LETHA *(chattily):* I sometimes know what you are going to think, dear. Remember the time I bought the bolt of silk from Cathay when you told me not to have that Syrian peddler in the house again, and I did it anyway, and you came in and—

PRIEST *(thunderously):* Letha!

LETHA *(quickly):* Well, anyway, I knew what you would think!

PRIEST: Girls, take your mother out.

MARUM: Oh, Father, please!

BEIRA: I shan't let her say another word. Please, Father.

PRIEST: Oh, all right. But this is the last warning. Now, about this innkeeper.

AZRA: At this very moment he is walking the street in front of this house. Be silent and Ubo and I shall summon him. *(All still. AZRA and UBO concentrate. Pause. INNKEEPER enters left, bewildered.)*

UBO: We did it!

INNKEEPER: I—I'm sorry! I—I don't know what possessed me!

AZRA: We did.

INNKEEPER: I meant no harm. I'll—I'll go at once.

PRIEST: Don't go. It's all right.

INNKEEPER *(looking at assembled group):* Am—am I dreaming?

AZRA: Don't be frightened. I am the angel Azra. Do you recognize that Man and the Samaritan?

INNKEEPER: Yes, but—for a moment I thought—*(Looks more closely at the two.)* They look—they look—why, they're *dead!* *(Alarmed.)*

AZRA: Yes. Don't be frightened. No harm will come to you. You were brought here to give your testimony.

INNKEEPER: *Brought* here?

UBO: Neat, wasn't it?

INNKEEPER: I—I just walked in! No one sent for me. And yet. I don't understand.

AZRA: Heaven can operate quite well without man's understanding. It asks only his trust. Now, we have some questions. Do you recognize this Samaritan?

INNKEEPER: Yes. For many years he was a regular guest at my inn. He was a travelling merchant and came my way a couple of times a year. I'm sorry to see you like this, sir!

SAMARITAN: Oh, I'm used to it.

INNKEEPER: The last time you were in my inn was when you brought this man to me. I expected you back.

SAMARITAN: I became very ill. I couldn't make that hard journey again. Then I died. Tell, me, did I owe you more?

INNKEEPER: No, sir. In fact, you paid me too much.

UBO: He *is* frightened.

PRIEST *(impatiently):* So the Innkeeper knows the Samaritan. What does that prove?

AZRA: Be patient. Innkeeper, this Samaritan brought you a man severely wounded?

INNKEEPER: Yes, that last time. It must have been twenty years ago. But there's the man. Ask him.

LEVITE: We have.

INNKEEPER: Well, then, you know how badly wounded he was. You wouldn't believe he could live. Not that the Samaritan hadn't already done as much as possible for him, cleaning and dressing his wounds. My wife said—

MARUM: Wife? Oh, dear!

BEIRA: Well, that's that.

INNKEEPER: My wife said his care saved the man's life. And when he arrived at the inn on the Samaritan's beast and covered with his cloak—

LEVITE: How do you know it was this Samaritan's cloak?

INNKEEPER: A Samaritan cloak is a Samaritan cloak. Besides he had worn it on other trips and I recognized it.

AZRA: Go on with your story.

INNKEEPER: Well, my Samaritan guest paid for the man's care until he should be able to travel again, and left him with me and my good wife. She has considerable skill as a nurse. He promised to pay additional cost when he came that way again. But he never did.

PRIEST: Why did you trust his word?

INNKEEPER: Why not? He stayed in my inn many times. I knew he was an honorable man.

PRIEST *(shocked):* A *Samaritan?*

INNKEEPER: Samaritan or Hebrew, it makes no difference to me what a man's race, so long as he pays his debts. I got over that fool-

76

ishness a long time ago. I am in the business of running an inn for money.

LEVITE: I never thought to hear a Hebrew speak well of a Samaritan!

INNKEEPER: Look. I *knew* him. If he were alive, I'd trust him now. Besides bread bought with Samaritan money tastes just like bread bought with Hebrew money. Anyway there's the man he brought in. He can tell you all I say is true.

MAN: They won't believe me because I was unconscious.

INNKEEPER: Unconscious? You were that! One nearer death I never hope to see, present company excepted. But the Samaritan and the physician and my good wife between them gave you back life. Well, for a while anyway.

MAN: Thank you again, my friend.

INNKEEPER: Oh, that's all right. It was the Samaritan who really saved your life.

AZRA: I believe that is all. Thank you for coming.

INNKEEPER: Don't thank me. Thank—whatever it was.

UBO: Me!

INNKEEPER *(to MAN and SAMARITAN):* Good-bye, my friends. *(Exit.)*

LEVITE *(to Priest):* Old friend, could we be mistaken? Could there be good in a Samaritan?

PRIEST: No! I will not admit I'm wrong. I will not back down now that death is near!

UBO *(sniff): Seven* now.

AZRA: Not even when you are proved wrong by these witnesses?

PRIEST *(angry):* I reject this "proof."

AZRA: Your acceptance is vital only to you. Ignoring God's laws does not nullify them. They continue to operate. However, in this rejection, you are losing your last chance to become a better human being. These are precious, fleeting moments. It is no use, I see. You will die as you have lived, a bigot.

PRIEST: I will not be insulted in my own house!

AZRA: No one is insulting you. You, yourself, are the insult.

LETHA *(she and daughters dash to couch):* Oh, my poor departing husband! How can he say such wicked things to you?

UBO: He forces himself.

MARUM: It is unkind.

BEIRA: Even if true.

PRIEST: Stay out of this.

LETHA: I only wanted to comfort you. *(To AZRA.)* See what you've done? You've made him angry and we try never to make him angry! Always we manage so that he will not be angry. It is bad for him.

MARUM: Because he yells.

BEIRA: And turns purple.

PRIEST: Shut up! Get out of the way! Get back! *(He shakes his fist. They retreat and subside.)*

AZRA: It was to no purpose, but we tried to make you understand. Knowing the man you are, we felt you wouldn't change, but heaven's mercy is extended to the hard of heart as well as the receptive. Heaven decrees, man vetoes. Come now.

PRIEST *(calmer):* I still don't remember, and I won't accept what I can't remember, in spite of what you say.

LEVITE: Never mind, old friend. You go with Ubo. I shall be with you some day. When I arrive, you can move into my mansion with me.

AZRA: *Your* mansion? You went across the road and looked at the wounded man. You clearly saw his mortal need, and turned away. Yours is the greater sin for your knowledge was greater. You will inherit, not a Class C dwelling, but a Class *D—one* window.

UBO *(sniff):* And a Class D angel isn't nearly as attractive as I am!

AZRA: It is time to go. In fact it is well past the time intended.

UBO: *Nine,* now. *(They all look at him.)* Well, I told you it was the busy season!

PRIEST: All right. All right! I suppose there's no changing things. *(He stands left of couch.)*

AZRA: Even now? *(He sees there's no hope.)*
LETHA *(rushes to PRIEST and throws her arms around him hysterically)*: Oh, husband, I shall miss you! No one from my youth to talk to, no one to share memories, no one to—

PRIEST *(desperately pushing her away)*: Heaven calls me!
MARUM *(LETHA and daughters go to stand by LEVITE, who comforts LETHA reluctantly)*: Father, don't forget us!

BEIRA *(matter-of-factly)*: We shall mourn for you the prescribed period.
PRIEST *(looking over his family)*: There are going to be compensations, after all. *(To LEVITE, emotionally.)* Farewell, old friend. I shall be waiting.

LEVITE: Don't look for me too soon!
UBO *(happily)*: Let's go. *(brisk sniff as he goes left with PRIEST behind him. AZRA also starts off with dead men behind him. All meet. PRIEST stops in injured dignity, bringing all to standstill.)*

UBO: Now what?
PRIEST *(sarcastically)*: By all means, let this—this *Samaritan*—leave first! *(To SAMARITAN.)* Go ahead! *(To AZRA.)* I trust this place to which I go is aware of the difference between me, a Hebrew, and this—*Samaritan!*

AZRA: Indeed, yes. He dwells in a mansion on the hill. You are not allowed up there.

PRIEST *(indignantly)*: What! Is there no justice in heaven?
AZRA: That's what it is—justice.

(They all depart. The LEVITE looks uncomfortable as he follows the women off in the other direction, and they begin formal wailing.)

THE END

THE BARRIER

CAST: MARY OF MAGDALA, *a young girl*
GAIUS CLAUDIUS SIXTUS, *a young Roman centurion*
MARY, *the mother of Jesus*
SALOME, *her older sister*
JOHN, *Salome's younger son, an apostle*
SIMON PETER, *an older apostle*
JOANNA, *a follower of Jesus, wife to Herod's steward*
VOICE OF JESUS, *heard offstage*

TIME: During the last years of Jesus' life and the persecution following his death.

COSTUMES: Entirely biblical, or in dark modern dress with appropriate biblical head coverings.

STAGING AND LIGHTING: Use three series of levels, left, right and center back. These levels can be circular, or square platforms, stacked one on the other or even the natural levels in the church. The center back levels are higher and wider than the other two. Each series of levels will have its own sharply defined spotlight, making transitions smooth, and aiding the illusion of passing time. The actors have no furniture, instead, they use the levels.

(Spot up on back levels. Peter, Salome and Mary-Mother re-

*vealed in arrested motion. Freeze a moment. Then Peter con-
tinues to top of levels. Mary-Mother sits, Salome continues into
scene from back as Joanna centers right.)*

JOANNA: Everything's ready.

SALOME: Except solving our problem. Mary of Magdala.

MARY-MOTHER: Now, Salome! Maybe John won't find Reuben.
Or—or maybe the moon will be too bright. Then we can't leave
tonight.

PETER *(strong, as he became after Jesus' death):* We must leave tonight, Mary.

SALOME *(sharply):* Then you must decide about Mary of Magdala
now! She won't just vanish to save you the trouble.

*(John, gasping harshly, runs into spot, collapses on levels. The
others, alarmed, hovering around him, all talk at once)*

SALOME: Son!

MARY-MOTHER: John!

JOANNA: Are you hurt?

PETER: What is it?

JOHN: Soldiers!

PETER *(running back to imaginary window, alarmed):* You brought
them here?

JOHN: No! I lost them!

PETER *(returning):* Are you sure?

JOHN *(still gasping):* Yes! I came over the roofs!

SALOME *(touching him here and there):* Are you hurt?

JOHN *(pushing her away):* No! Oh, mother, let me alone.

JOANNA: What happened?

JOHN: I don't know. From nowhere, Roman soldiers and Temple
Guards. Shouting at me. I ran. Just luck I got away.

MARY-MOTHER: We must thank Jehovah.

PETER: What about Reuben? You found him?

JOHN *(breathing easier, nods):* Reuben and Abiram will get us over
the wall near the Gennath Gate.

PETER: But there are soldiers there. Why not elsewhere?

JOHN: The best cover is there. Abiram's daughter will take her little brothers to the gate to create a diversion.

PETER: Children? You trust children?

JOHN: These children, yes. They'll say another brother was locked outside the gate. The Romans will rightly refuse to open it. Five screaming, yelling children can create enough diversion! We won't be noticed or heard.

MARY-MOTHER: Suppose something goes wrong?

JOHN: It won't. James and the others reached Capernaum. We will, too, Aunt Mary.

PETER: As long as we stay off the roads.

MARY-MOTHER *(coming to Peter):* I'm so afraid. Let me stay here.

JOANNA: No place in Jerusalem is safe now, Mary.

PETER *(patting Mary's hand comfortingly):* You just keep on thinking about reaching Capernaum.

SALOME: I wish you had more backbone, Mary!

PETER: And I wish you had more charity, Salome.

JOHN *(savagely, aside to Peter):* If those—animals—out there knew that Jesus' mother was in here—

PETER: John! The women will need all their courage.

JOANNA: I'll be glad to leave here. This house has become a prison.

JOHN: Someday we'll come back, Joanna. Free.

SALOME: If we live.

PETER: We must.

JOANNA *(looking out imaginary window):* It's growing dark.

JOHN *(suddenly missing her):* Where is Mary of Magdala?

JOANNA: She took bread to Thomas of Gaza, hiding under the old fish market.

JOHN *(alarmed):* You sent her out there, Joanna?

JOANNA: Well, someone had to go.

JOHN: Mother, why did you let her go?

SALOME: I'm not her keeper! Besides, *she's* safe, if anyone is!

JOHN *(ominously):* All right, Mother! Joanna, does she know we're leaving tonight?

JOANNA: No.

JOHN *(starting off):* I'll go look for her.

SALOME: Where's your pride? She's probably with that Roman again. You don't see proper *Jewish* girls taking up with Romans!

JOHN *(sullenly):* I'm not interested in proper Jewish girls. At least *he* won't be in Capernaum.

JOANNA: Peter, we must decide before she returns. Will we take her with us to Capernaum? Or leave her in Magdala?

SALOME: Leave her in Magdala!

JOHN: Magdala? Mother, what's this about?

SALOME: We might as well face it. Mary of Magdala will never be anything but a handicap to us from now on.

MARY-MOTHER: Now, Salome.

SALOME: Don't "Now Salome" me! You know what happens every time we say, "This is Mary of Magdala!"

MARY-MOTHER: Oh.

SALOME: "Oh" is right. Everybody knows about the women of Magdala. With Magdala so near the garrison in Tiberias! A disgrace! I am embarrassed to say "Magdala" before my sons.

PETER: Then don't. You talk too much anyway.

JOHN: Mother, James and I have known about Magdala since we were boys.

SALOME: From hanging around those fishermen with your father, no doubt.

PETER: I am one of those fishermen, Salome. I have faults. But never Magdala.

SALOME: Well, anyway people talk about her.

JOHN: You know they are wrong. Do you ever try to stop them?

SALOME: I don't "know" any such thing. Besides they'd talk anyway. Wherever we went. With her along. *(Aside to women.)* Do you want people to think that about us?

JOANNA: At *our* age? Not likely!

JOHN: Mother! Jesus said—

SALOME: Oh, we all know what Jesus said! Just the same, I've always been suspicious of her.

JOANNA: And jealous? She's young, beautiful. And John likes her.

SALOME *(scoffing):* A Greek from Magdala? Ha! John's too young to know what he likes.

JOHN: I can speak for myself.

MARY-MOTHER: Salome, if she were an ugly Jewess would you forgive her for growing up in Magdala?

SALOME: Mary, don't be so smug! Even you were suspicious of her at first.

(Spot up on right levels where Mary-Magdala stands motionless)

I remember the day she came. Right here in Jerusalem.

(All freeze in place. Spot dims slowly. All shift to new positions for flashback section. Mary-Mother joins Mary-Magdala. Spot fades on right and slowly comes up again on center back as Mary-Mother brings Mary-Magdala to meet the others. Each responds with "Mary" or "Shalom.")

MARY-MOTHER: Here is someone Jesus wants you to meet. Mary, these are Jesus' friends. Simon. Joanna. My sister, Salome, and her son, John. Mary is from—Magdala. *(Dismayed reactions. Salome says it all.)*

SALOME: *Magdala!*

MARY-MOTHER *(hastily):* Jesus wants Mary to go with us to Galilee.

PETER *(the early impulsive Simon):* He can't! I'll go tell him right now! *(He starts off.)*

MARY-MOTHER: Wait, Simon! He has already decided. You know Jesus.

PETER *(Returns, disgruntled.)* Why does he pick up such people? *(Looks the girl over. Her head shawl is around her shoulders, her hair uncovered.)* Well, girl! Don't you know how to dress around decent people?

MARY-MAGDALA *(covers hair):* I—I forget Jewish ways.
PETER *(dismayed):* You're not a Jew?

MARY-MAGDALA *(nervously):* Half Jewish. My—my father was Greek.
PETER: A Gentile and a Magdalene! What will we do with her? Can she help you women?

SALOME *(with a sniff):* Not likely.
JOANNA *(examining Mary's hands):* No callouses. Don't you do any useful work, girl?

MARY-MAGDALA: Oh, yes. But I've been—ill. A long time. My mind—
MARY-MOTHER: Jesus cured her. He said there were devils in her head.
SALOME: Oh?
PETER *(grudgingly):* I suppose we'll have to take you along if Jesus says so. See that you behave yourself, girl!

(Peter and the other women go aside to discuss the unwelcome addition in pantomime. John joins Mary-Magdala.)

JOHN: Don't worry. They aren't so bad.
MARY-MAGDALA: They don't want me.
JOHN: Magdala sticks in their throats. They just can't believe—well, they'll do what Jesus says even if they don't want to. You know, you look more Greek than Jewish. *(They continue talking in pantomime.)*

SALOME *(watching them):* I think we'd better watch her.
JOANNA: So do I. For different reasons.
MARY-MOTHER *(gentle complaint):* Sometimes Jesus gets carried away!

(Spot off large levels, up on left levels. On top, Gaius the centurion sees Mary-Magdala, face uncovered, coming along the "street." Intercepts her.)

GAIUS: Girl! Girl! *(She covers face, tries to pass. He grasps her arm.)* It *is* you. Remember me?

MARY-MAGDALA *(frightened):* Yes! Let me go! *(Struggles.)*

GAIUS *(harshly):* Stand still, girl! Unless you want a scene right here on the street! That's better. Now, listen to me. It wasn't entirely my fault we got off to a bad start in Magdala. You can't blame me. What was I to think? Why was a girl like you in Magdala anyway?

MARY-MAGDALA *(angry):* That shopkeeper was my uncle!

GAIUS: The Greek I knocked down? Too bad. When I saw you in that shop—naturally I thought—well, it seems I was wrong.

MARY-MAGDALA *(trying to pass):* It doesn't matter.

GAIUS *(blocking her):* Hold on! It matters to me. I went back to that shop twice to say I was sorry but the place was closed. Now I'm going to say it. So you listen! You won't often hear an apology from a Roman.

MARY-MAGDALA: All right. I forgive you. Is that all?

GAIUS *(looking her over):* I don't understand it. Why do I thank the gods our paths crossed today? You are rude, ill-mannered. I've known a lot of girls more beautiful than you are. Yet you are the one I can't forget.

MARY-MAGDALA: Try harder. Shalom.

GAIUS: Wait! I don't even know your name. I could follow you to find out.

MARY-MAGDALA *(quickly):* It's Mary!

GAIUS: Mine's Gaius. Gaius Claudius Sixtus.

MARY-MAGDALA: I believe you. Please let me go now.

GAIUS *(demandingly):* When will I see you again?

MARY-MAGDALA: Never. A respectable Jewish woman doesn't talk to Romans.

GAIUS: But—you're Greek!

MARY-MAGDALA: Only half. Shalom.

(She moves to go. He puts out a hand to detain her. John rushes angrily into spot, pulls Mary behind him. Scene moves rapidly.)

JOHN: Don't touch her, Roman!

GAIUS *(as they struggle)*: Out of my way, fellow!

MARY-MAGDALA *(pushing between them)*: Stop it! John, I know him! Stop it!

(Surprised, John stops, Gaius lets go, Mary separates them.)

JOHN *(furiously)*: This—this *Roman?*

GAIUS *(contemptuously)*: Yes, Jew! This Roman.

(He pulls Mary to him, John springs at him, Mary separates them again.)

GAIUS: You dare attack a Roman?

MARY-MAGDALA: Don't blame him! He's one of my people!

GAIUS: Then get him away.

JOHN: You leave her alone, Roman!

MARY-MAGDALA: Come on, John. Let's go find Jesus.

GAIUS *(insolently)*: Jesus? Another of your Jewish friends?

MARY-MAGDALA: Come away, John. Please.

GAIUS *(hand on Mary's shoulder)*: Why the haste? A friendly re-union—

JOHN *(pushing his hand away)*: Keep your hand off her, Roman!

MARY-MAGDALA: John! What will Jesus say?

GAIUS: Well, Jew, it seems you're afraid of this Jesus, whoever he is.

JOHN: Messiah! Son of Jehovah!

GAIUS: Ah! Now I know. You're with that fanatic from Galilee. *(Laughs.)* Oh, Mary! Not you, too?

(Spot off quickly and up on right levels, revealing Peter, shocked at what he sees.)

PETER *(calling)*: John! Mary! *(They come to him, Mary covering her face.)* John, go to Jesus at once. He's in the Temple. Mary, stay here.

JOHN: Now Simon don't blame Mary! It was that Roman.

PETER: Go on! *(John leaves reluctantly. Peter turns on Mary furiously.)* Do you know the penalty for striking a Roman?

MARY-MAGDALA *(defensively):* I tried—

PETER: I saw you talking to that Roman, your face uncovered!

MARY-MAGDALA: I forgot.

PETER: Dragging John into a fight!

MARY-MAGDALA: I didn't ask him to interfere!

PETER: Besides you bring shame on the Master. You and your Greek ways.

MARY-MAGDALA: It's hard to remember all the time!

PETER: For—a Magdalene?

MARY-MAGDALA: You sound like Salome.

PETER: Salome's a good woman. She wants the best for her sons. If you weren't from Magdala—

MARY-MAGDALA: Then it would be something else. For Jesus' sake I try to treat all of you the same. Tell her to keep her precious John away!

PETER: You failed to learn many things a Jewish girl learns. One is good manners.

MARY-MAGDALA: You think only Jews are perfect? My uncle was a good man. As long as he lived he took good care of me!

PETER: That's hard to believe.

MARY-MAGDALA: You mean— Oh, that's it, isn't it, Simon? Do you think the Master *lied* about me? All right I'll say it. Jesus cured my mind, not my morals! I never was a harlot! Never, never, never!

PETER *(shocked):* Mary! No proper Jewish girl would speak so coarsely. We won't mention the subject again.

MARY-MAGDALA *(near tears):* Oh, Simon.

PETER: Come on. The Master asked for you. We leave for Galilee.

MARY-MAGDALA *(covers face as she follows, pleading)*: Please, Simon. Listen. I'm sorry. Please, Simon. Please listen.

(Exeunt. Spot off slowly. Hold darkness few seconds. Then spot up left as slowly. Mary-Mother and Joanna seated.)

JOANNA *(sighs)*: I don't remember when I've been so tired.

MARY-MOTHER *(wearily)*: All the years of traveling.

JOANNA: I could stand the traveling. I think it's the friction these last months.

MARY-MOTHER: Poor Mary. And poor Salome. She never changes.

JOANNA: I tell her not to worry. Mary's not in love with John.

MARY-MOTHER: She can't believe any girl John likes can resist him, and Mary has been around so long now. Well, Salome can't interest John in any other girl.

JOANNA: Salome takes motherhood harder than most.

MARY-MOTHER: I'll be glad to leave Jerusalem again. If Jesus weren't so particular about this Passover. *(Stands, looks off.)* Where is Mary? I sent her for the wine. She should be back. I'll go see if she's coming. *(Starts down levels.)*

JOANNA: I'd better get on with preparations. Come help when you can. *(Leaves the other way.)*

(Mary-Mother watches. Soon Mary-Magdala runs to her, agitated.)

MARY-MOTHER: Where have you been? Where is the wine?

MARY-MAGDALA: I didn't get it!

MARY-MOTHER: Oh, Mary! Now, I'll have to go myself.

MARY-MAGDALA: No, no! Come inside! Get off the street.

MARY-MOTHER: What's wrong?

MARY-MAGDALA: I'm afraid. In the streets I heard terrible things against the Master!

MARY-MOTHER: Is that all? Jesus does stir people up, as you know.

MARY-MAGDALA: I must tell him!

MARY-MOTHER: No, you won't. He has enough problems already.

89

MARY-MAGDALA: Suppose they try to harm him?

MARY-MOTHER: Oh, Mary, this is a holy time. Jesus is safe in Jerusalem at Passover, surely. In a few days we'll return to Galilee. Go help Johanna. I'll get the wine. Go on, now!

MARY-MAGDALA *(follows Mary-Mother to edge of spot)*: Be careful! *(The Mother is gone. Mary speaks to herself)* No one listens to Mary of Magdala! *(Sees someone approaching.)* A Roman! Simon will be angry! *(Turns away, motionless to escape notice.)*

GAIUS: Mary? Mary, is it you?

MARY-MAGDALA: Gaius!

(They meet. He takes her hands.)

MARY-MAGDALA: I—I must go in at once.

GAIUS: I've been walking all over this part of Jerusalem looking for you. I heard the Nazarene was back and I knew—

MARY-MAGDALA *(freeing hands)*: I—I must go help with the Passover supper.

GAIUS: Mary, please! It's been nearly a year.

MARY-MAGDALA *(softly)*: I know.

GAIUS: You are still running away from me.

MARY-MAGDALA: You know I can't stay.

GAIUS *(significantly)*: So *this* is where the Galilean is? Your Sanhedrin would pay a nice reward for that information, I'm thinking.

MARY-MAGDALA: You wouldn't!

GAIUS: Not if you will talk to me. Come over here, Mary. *(They sit.)* All year long I thought of things to tell you. Now that you're here—well, they've all gone. I might begin with—how is that friendly fellow, John?

MARY-MAGDALA *(as they both laugh)*: He doesn't like you either.

GAIUS: I know why. I don't think I wish him *ill* exactly. But I can't say honestly I wish him well either. If your friends are all like John—Mary, why do you stay with them?

MARY-MAGDALA: Because of Jesus. I owe him so much. When my uncle died—

GAIUS: I didn't hurt him that much!

MARY-MAGDALA: No, no. He opened a shop here in Jerusalem to get away from Magdala. Then—a wasting sickness. After he died I fell ill of a fever. My body recovered, but my mind—I don't remember. They say I saw visions and things beyond the world of men. When Jesus found me, I was in the hands of my masters. I'd become a dancer. My masters—Oh, Gaius it is terrible to think of the things they say I said and did, all unknowing. One possessed. Now it is all like a dream that happened to someone else.

GAIUS: Don't think of it.

MARY-MAGDALA: But that's why I stay with the followers of Jesus. He gave me back to myself. He is so good. No one I ever knew is so good.

GAIUS: So good that your own leaders, that Sanhedrin, are after him? They don't like what he says about them. They are busy stirring up the crowds against him, all those here for your Passover. Pilate may have to arrest your Jesus.

MARY-MAGDALA: If Pilate knows this, why doesn't he arrest the Sanhedrin?

GAIUS: Don't be naive, Mary. Some of those men are rich and powerful. Your Jesus is only a peasant, a local agitator.

MARY-MAGDALA: You don't know him. Gaius, will you come meet him?

GAIUS: Some day, perhaps. You might tell him a Roman sends a warning: get out of Jerusalem.

MARY-MAGDALA: I told his mother what I heard in the streets. She insists he's safe during Passover.

GAIUS: She's wrong. None of you with him is safe either. It wouldn't take much for a mob. Mary, won't you leave here? Go to Tiberias or even Magdala.

MARY-MAGDALA: I can't do that.

GAIUS: I don't care about the threats to the Nazarene. But I don't want anything to happen to you. Listen, Mary. I'm not a man for pretty speeches. So, I'll say it straight out. Mary, I love you.

MARY-MAGDALA: That—That's impossible! You—you don't know me. Not really.

GAIUS: More than you realize. Since that unfortunate day in Magdala, I've not been able to get you out of my thoughts. Oh, I've tried! But there you stayed. I went back to Magdala twice this year hunting for you.

MARY-MAGDALA *(agitated):* But Gaius—

GAIUS: Mary, so far I've not given you any reason to—like me. But, we can't go back and start over. Do you think, can we pretend *this* is the beginning?

MARY-MAGDALA: Gaius, this must be the ending.

GAIUS: Do you dislike me so much?

MARY-MAGDALA: Oh, no, Gaius!

GAIUS *(arms around her):* In time you will love me, Mary.

MARY-MAGDALA: No, Gaius, I can't let myself care for you.

GAIUS: Nonsense! Some day—

MARY-MAGDALA: *(pushing him away):* Never. You are a pagan. I am a follower of Jesus.

GAIUS *(jealous):* What's his hold over you? All right, I admit I'm jealous! He's a man, isn't he?

MARY-MAGDALA: Not like other men.

GAIUS: Why not?

MARY-MAGDALA: He's Messiah, the Holy One of Israel, Son of Jehovah.

GAIUS: Maybe he is. Roman gods beget sons. In our house your Jehovah can have equal place with Jove and Apollo.

MARY-MAGDALA *(turning away):* No, Gaius.

GAIUS *(angry):* You want to waste your life on that Nazarene?

MARY-MAGDALA: It's not waste!

GAIUS: Oh, isn't it? What kind of girl will give up love to wander around with a fanatic who says he's the son of an invisible God?

MARY-MAGDALA: Oh, go away! You'll never understand. Leave me alone!

GAIUS: All right, I will! *(Leaves angrily.)*

MARY-MAGDALA: Don't come back! Oh, Gaius, I—I didn't mean it.

(Freezes briefly. Hears following offstage and reacts.)

VOICE *(off)*: Someone will betray me. One of you here.

(Murmurs of shock and protest with these speeches topping.)

PETER *(off)*: Lord, you don't think I could—? Oh, Master, you don't believe that?

JOHN *(off)*: Oh, Master, surely not I? I would never betray you!

VOICE *(off)*: He knows his name.

(Spot off left and up on right levels. Peter is seen, prostrate in grief. For a time he doesn't move. When he does a soft drum beat is heard. Groaning, face down, he punctuates each "why" by striking the floor with his fist. Simultaneous drum beat. A kettle drum is ideal for this and for the thunder later. This scene should have long silences.)

PETER: Oh, why? Why? Why? Why?

(He is motionless again. Soon Mary-Magdala enters slowly, heart-broken. Sees Peter, thinks he's hurt. Kneels by him, alarmed.)

MARY-MAGDALA: Simon! Simon, are you hurt?

(He stirs but doesn't answer. She rises.)

MARY-MAGDALA: Wait! Ill go for help.

PETER: No! Don't leave me, Mary I need you. You understand.

MARY-MAGDALA *(sits beside him)*: Do I, Simon? Understand what?

PETER: Sin. Oh, Mary! Mary.

MARY-MAGDALA *(helps him sit up)*: What's wrong, Simon?

PETER *(groaning)*: Jesus—

MARY-MAGDALA *(frightened):* Oh, he's not—
PETER: No! Mary—I—I— *(He can't say it.)*
MARY-MAGDALA: Tell me, Simon.
PETER: I said—I said—I—didn't know him. They *recognized* me, Mary! I denied even knowing him! To the soldiers. And the common women in that courtyard.

MARY-MAGDALA: Oh, Simon!
PETER *(head in hands):* I—I was afraid.
MARY-MAGDALA: We're all afraid. Sometime. Even the bravest.
PETER *(near tears):* He—he heard me! He looked straight at me! Oh, Master! *(He breaks down as she tries to comfort him.)*

(Spot fades slowly. In brief darkness, all gather around large levels: Peter, Mary-Magdala, Salome and Joanna one side; John, Mary-Mother the other. Gaius near top center. Sounds of grief, sobs, murmurs. Just enough light up so figures are seen dimly. Sounds of thunder, flickers of lightning throughout, continuing until we hear the following.)

VOICE *(off):* Father! Forgive them! *(Loud thunder, bright lightning.)* I come to you, Father! *(Loud thunder, bright lightning.)*

(Silence. Softer thunder and lightning. Sounds of grief.)

GAIUS *(awed):* He—really was—the Son of God!

(Spot off slowly. Dying thunder stops. Then spot up slowly on right levels where Joanna, Salome, Mary-Magdala sit, dim at first then brightening. Tempo of scene is slow, subdued.)

MARY-MAGDALA *(dully):* It soon will be light. Then we can go on.
JOANNA *(after pause):* It's so lonely out here. Do you think the storm is coming back?

MARY-MAGDALA: The thunder was dying.
SALOME: How will we move the heavy stone from the entrance?
MARY-MAGDALA: Perhaps the Roman soldiers guarding the tomb will help.
JOANNA: I don't like to ask them.

SALOME: I know. The way Romans look at us.

JOANNA: Not at *us*, Salome. Not for some years. At Mary.

SALOME: Then let Mary ask. She seems to have a way with Romans!

JOANNA: Now, Salome!

SALOME: Mary knows by now I say what I think.

JOANNA: Then stop thinking.

MARY-MAGDALA: We can see now.

(They rise, walk slowly to large levels, which are in light now. See no soldiers. Light off right levels.)

MARY-MAGDALA: Where are the soldiers?

(See tomb is open, are frightened.)

JOANNA: Look! It's open! *(They huddle together.)*

SALOME: I don't see anyone around. Not a soldier. Let's look inside.

(They go up and peer into imaginary tomb.)

JOANNA *(shocked)*: Jesus is gone!

SALOME: The Romans have stolen him!

MARY-MAGDALA: Why?

SALOME: Who knows? But he's gone. *(Mary sits, weeping.)*

JOANNA: We must tell Simon and the others. Come on. *(Joanna and Salome run off, leaving Mary weeping.)*

VOICE *(off)*: Mary.

(She looks toward Voice. "Sees" Jesus. A look of pure joy as she holds out her hands to him. An amazed whisper, then a great cry of joy.)

MARY-MAGDALA: Master? *Master!*

(Spot off large levels and up slowly on left. Gaius waits. Mary runs in from right. He speaks before she can tell him.)

GAIUS: How can you bear the sight of me? That cross! I looked up into the face of *God!* These hands. His blood. I killed him.

MARY-MAGDALA: He's alive!

GAIUS *(unhearing):* "Father, forgive them." That's what he said. He forgave *me.* I'll never forgive myself!

MARY-MAGDALA *(shakes his arm):* Gaius, listen to me! He's alive!

GAIUS: A soldier knows the sight of death. Denying won't undo it.

MARY-MAGDALA: It's true. He's alive. I saw him. He spoke to me.

GAIUS: Alive? If I could believe that—Oh, Mary! Make me believe! *(She puts her arms around him. Spot off slowly. A brief pause, then spot up on right. Mary-Magdala sits with head on drawn up knees. Then Joanna enters spot.)*

JOANNA: Mary, I need you. Are you all right?

MARY-MAGDALA: All right, Joanna. Just tired.

JOANNA: I know. These terrible days. Well, we're alive. Mary, the soldiers are out again, searching out Jesus' followers. Thomas of Gaza is hiding in the cellar under the old fish market. Thirteen with him. Some children. They need bread. There's no one else to send.

MARY-MAGDALA *(wearily):* I'll go.

JOANNA: Be careful. *(Mary doesn't move.)* Mary! They need the bread now! What's the matter with you?

MARY-MAGDALA: Why did it all turn out this way, Joanna? First Jesus. Then afterward we grew strong for a time, didn't we? Why did Jehovah let us grow strong, Joanna? All those secure months. Then this terror. Why, Joanna?

JOANNA: Stop it, Mary!

MARY-MAGDALA: Stephen. All those others. The running. The hiding in cellars. .

JOANNA *(shakes her shoulder):* Stop thinking of what you can't change! Take the bread now. And don't stop to see your Roman.

MARY-MAGDALA: I haven't seen him in two weeks.

JOANNA: Good.

MARY-MAGDALA: He's been in Jericho. I couldn't.

JOANNA: Mary, forget your Roman lover. You are a follower of Jesus. He is a pagan.

MARY-MAGDALA: You don't know, Joanna. None of you know. Gaius doesn't want me to tell you yet.

JOANNA: Take the bread. Be sure no one follows you back here.
MARY-MAGDALA: By this time, I know all the secret ways.

(Joanna exits right. Mary covers her face and goes left. Spot slowly fades on right and comes up on left. Mary-Magdala slips into spot and waits for Gaius to pass. When he does, she calls.)

MARY-MAGDALA: Gaius!
GAIUS *(they embrace):* Mary! Why are you here?
MARY-MAGDALA: To see you.

GAIUS: A foolish risk. Get back in the shadows. *(They step back.)* What if you are seen?
MARY-MAGDALA *(amused):* A woman with a Roman soldier near the barracks? Ah, Gaius, how you have changed.

GAIUS: This is no matter for jest, Mary. It's your life.
MARY-MAGDALA: You are my life. You've been gone two whole weeks, Gaius.
GAIUS *(embraces her):* It seemed more like two months. But this is dangerous. Why didn't you wait? I'd have come to you.

MARY-MAGDALA: Perhaps too late. We're leaving for Capernaum at any time. Even tonight.

GAIUS: Mary, don't go with them. Marry me now. We can go to Rome. As the wife of a Roman citizen, you'd be safe there. I promise you would.

MARY-MAGDALA: But Gaius—
GAIUS: There's no obstacle now. We love each other. I'm tired of waiting. We can't live apart. Either you must come with me—or I must go with you. *(Expressive groan.)* And—them.

MARY-MAGDALA *(delighted):* Oh, Gaius, would you? But—the army—

GAIUS: I'll give it up.

MARY-MAGDALA: What if later—You're not doing this just for me?

GAIUS *(thoughtfully):* No. Rather for this—*wonder*—which has happened to me. Although I *would* do it for you. I've been thinking about it for some time. *(Laughs.)* I must be mad! I can just see the faces of those Jews when this Roman—Mary, will they accept me?

MARY-MAGDALA: *I* accept you!

GAIUS: It's a bit different. They aren't in love with me. Especially John.

(They laugh, embrace. Spot off. Spot on large levels up slowly. Characters posed as when flashback began: Mary-Mother, Joanna, Peter, John, Salome. All freeze while Salome repeats lines she said earlier)

SALOME: Mary, don't be so smug! Even you were suspicious of her at first. Why, I remember the day she came. Right here in Jerusalem. *(All relax, come alive as she continues.)* We know she'll never be a proper Jewish girl.

JOHN *(moodily):* Along side of Mary, a proper Jewish girl is like—like watered milk!

SALOME *(to others):* You see? What did I tell you? She's corrupted my son with her Greek ways! The next thing, he'll be wanting her for a wife.

JOHN: I do. She won't have me.

SALOME *(angered at John's rejection by any girl):* There! She prefers that pagan Roman to a fine Jewish lad! Like to like, I say.

PETER: Salome, you've said enough. We know how you feel about Mary.

SALOME: Men! Always defending a pretty face. A face she shows in the public street, talking free and easy with men, like that Roman she slips out to meet, thinking we don't always know! Well, now he can go see her in Magdala!

JOHN: I won't let you leave her in Magdala. If Jesus were here you wouldn't even consider it.

PETER: If he were here, it wouldn't be necessary.
JOHN: What's the matter with all of you? You are talking about deserting a warm, tender woman who has shared your lives for nearly three years.

PETER: She grew up there. There are people she will know. But if that's the way you feel, stay in Magdala with her.

JOHN: If she'd have me! *(Groans.)* You know I can't. For me the command of the Master comes first. Peter, you meant that to hurt, didn't you?

PETER: To make you face facts. The fact is right now a Magdalene is a barrier to our purpose. A barrier so high we can't climb over. John, I don't enjoy hurting Mary, whatever our differences have been.

MARY-MOTHER *(coming to John)*: Forgive us, John.
JOHN *(bitterly)*: Forgive *you?* What right have I to forgive you, when I am letting her down?

SALOME: She's young. She'll get over it. She'll be *home*. And out of our hands.

JOHN *(wretchedly)*: It comes down to this: do we really forgive? We say the words. But deep down do we ever really forgive?

(Mary-Magdala and Gaius enter the scene. They are unaware of conflicting emotions.)

PETER: Mary! Do you betray us?

(Salome, Joanna, Mary-Mother quickly stand behind Peter and John.)

JOHN: Why are you here, Roman?

JOANNA: Oh, Mary, what have you done?

MARY-MAGDALA: Don't be afraid! Gaius is not an enemy. Truly. Believe me.

PETER: Then why is he here?

MARY-MAGDALA *(happily):* Peter, John, listen. We have come to tell you Gaius is a believer! Ever since—the hill.

PETER: A Gentile?

JOHN: You think that makes him welcome here?

MARY-MAGDALA: Oh, I hope so, John. He's giving up the army. He's coming with us to Capernaum. *(Silence.)* What's the matter? *(Silence.)* Don't you want him?

GAIUS *(harshly):* I told you, Mary.

MARY-MAGDALA: I won't go to Capernaum without him!

SALOME *(bluntly):* You're not going to Capernaum.

MARY-MAGDALA: Not—going—?

SALOME: We're leaving you in Magdala.

MARY-MAGDALA: But Salome, don't you *see?* This changes everything. I know Magdala has been a handicap for all of you. But now I won't be Mary of Magdala. I'll be Mary, wife of Gaius!

SALOME: A *Roman?* The very Roman who crucified the Master?

GAIUS: Come away, Mary.

PETER *(sadly):* Salome is right. *This* Roman does not help matters.

MARY-MAGDALA: Don't say that.

PETER: People always know. Our mission would be lost. This may be an unjust decision. I am not wise enough to know now. But it is necessary at this time.

MARY-MAGDALA: Oh, Gaius. Oh, Gaius!

GAIUS *(his arm around her):* It will be all right, Mary, darling.

JOHN *(scornfully):* Peter, do you really think Jesus expects *us* to go out and win a world for him?

GAIUS: What world? This narrow, self-righteous little world of Jews? Open your eyes, you who call yourselves his followers! Outside, there's a bigger world. Filled with Romans and Greeks and Thracians and Ethiopians! Yes, and Gaiuses and Marys! Out there you'll search a long time to find a Jew!

JOANNA: Jesus was a Jew!

GAIUS *(angrily)*: You'd imprison him in that flesh? Oh, no! Not the Jesus I found on that hill! Maybe it is fortunate he died. If you want his death to count for nothing, stay in your little Jewish corner!

MARY-MAGDALA *(brokenly)*: Let's go, Gaius.

MARY-MOTHER *(puts arms around Mary)*: Jesus loved you. Hold on to that thought, Mary. Forgive us.

GAIUS: As you forgave her? What kind of forgiveness is that? Forgiving the sin and rejecting the sinner? Even a Roman is more generous. Come, Mary.

JOHN: Mary, we'll take you to Magdala. You have friends. You needn't go with this Roman.

MARY-MAGDALA *(sadly)*: This Roman seems to be the only one who really wants me.

GAIUS: Mary is no longer your concern. We'll go together and take your Jesus to Rome. The Romans there never heard of him. They never heard of Magdala either. They'll accept Mary for what she truly is.

(They leave. Those left can't look at each other. The silence is broken by Salome in a weak imitation of her old manner.)

SALOME: Well! What can you expect from a Magdalene and a Roman!

JOANNA: Were we wrong?

SALOME: We did what was necessary! We have a mission. We removed a barrier.

PETER: Did we? Or is the barrier only higher? If Jesus were here—

JOHN *(bitterly):* If he were here? If he were here now, I wonder what he would say to us? What about the tomorrows and the tomorrows? How can he trust us now?

MARY-MOTHER: He has to. We are all he left.

THE END

VEIL TO TREASON

Title taken from: "Oh, treacherous night! thou lendest thy ready veil to every treason, and teeming mischiefs thrive beneath thy shade."—*Aaron Hill, English Dramatist* (1685-1750)

PRODUCTION NOTES

CHARACTERS: VOICE *of Jesus, never seen*
JUDAS *of Kerioth*
CHORUS: six men, four women. *the CHORUS acts at times as narrators. All are part of the crowd following John the Baptist, and later a casual crowd in Jerusalem. The* MEN *are the Sanhedrin. In addition,* MAN 1 *is Andrew;* MAN 2 *Simon Peter;* MAN 3, *Philip and John;* MAN 4, *Nathanael and James;* MAN 5, *Caiaphas; MAN 6, Annas.*

SETTING: *empty stage or sanctuary platform*

PROPS: *for JUDAS*, a bundle with bread, a leather pouch or wallet, and another small leather pouch with loose coins.
Two stools within easy access of actors (behind choir rail perhaps).

COSTUMES: If biblical—*JUDAS*: heavy, long brown tunic, lighter shade girdle or sash which can wrap around his body several times, sandals or barefoot. If his hair is long, no headdress. If short, a small turban. *CHORUS*: identical tunics, a lighter shade than Judas', with self girdles. Small turbans for men and identical headscarves for women, same material. All sandals or all barefoot. Optional beards for men.

If modern: *CHORUS*, black sweaters and slacks or skirts. *JUDAS*: brown sweater and slacks. He must have a long cummerbund, wrapped around and around, even with modern clothes.

LIGHTING SUGGESTIONS: These lighting suggestions can aid the production. Use as many lights as possible. The average church has an arched or vaulted front. Against that wall, place light which will be directed up against that wall only, such as a string of Christmas lights behind a shield of cardboard. With other lights off, this gives the silhouette effect for the Sanhedrin scenes. Arrange other lights to illuminate the entire stage. Finally, a moving spot for Judas, with blue-violet, red, and night blue frames. For the flickering torch effect: a small electric fan with paper streamers fastened. Place fan on its back in front of the spotlight. Use a dimmer where available; if not, a shield slid over a light gives a dimming effect. When the play opens, the stage is all lighted and Judas' spot has the blue-violet filter.

(Judas enters left, carrying his bundle. Sits on floor down front left, begins to eat. Chorus, except Man 1, now a crowd following John the Baptist, enters right, excited, talking at once. Judas eavesdrops, interested.)

CHORUS *(overlapping ad lib)*: Saw you the anger of the old one?
The small one shouted with such fury his own words choked him!
Saw you their surprise at our number?
Aye! Unwelcome surprise!
The Baptist stood firm against them.
He was not afraid!

MAN 1 *(running in from left)*: Is it true? A committee from the Council at Jerusalem—the Sanhedrin—to see the Baptist?

104

CHORUS *(variously, overlapping):* Oh, yes. Indeed. True. Aye!

WOMAN 1 *(over all):* Why were not you with us?

MAN 2: Could you but have seen him face them! *(All assent.)*

MAN 1 *(worried):* Why Jerusalem's interest in the Baptist?

MAN 3: Because of a tale-bearer, no doubt. The Council heard that the Baptist spoke against them.

CHORUS *(indignantly, overlapping):* Untrue. Never did he so speak. A lie. Such words we never heard!

MAN 4 *(loudly overlapping):* Also, 'tis said, we call the Baptist the promised Christ, the King of Israel!

JUDAS *(hunger forgotten, enthralled):* King? King? *(None answer him.)*

CHORUS *(variously, overlapping):* They are filled with fears. Why must they tell lies? Is it the Romans they fear?

MAN 1: So the Sanhedrin sends a committee?

WOMAN 2: Five of them. Rich men. Such handsome robes. *(To another.)* Saw you the shining stone in the fat one's ring? A fortune!

WOMAN 3: And servants!

MAN 1: Oh, that I had been there.

WOMAN 4 *(beginning to set out scene):* There was the Baptist, there by the river. And here we were, watching and listening. Suddenly rich strangers came upon us. Their servants pushed us aside to clear a way for their masters.

MAN 4 *(holding his nose):* Lest we offend their Jerusalem noses! *(All laugh.)*

105

WOMAN 4 *(continuing. She pushes others, even Judas, aside. All enter into mimicry)*: Aye! These lords must not walk too close to common people!

MAN 3 *(overacting, indicating he is a large man with a big stomach, pompous. Addresses* MAN 4 *whom* WOMAN 4 *Selects to play John the Baptist.)*: Disturbing reports reach us in the Sanhedrin. The—ah—Council has sent us from Jerusalem. Ah—what means this idle crowd? Why gather you here? Ah—have you nothing better to do? No children to tend? No bread to earn? Ah—what if the Roman officials hear of this multitude? *(To "John.")* You encourage their folly! 'Tis said you call yourself the Holy One of Israel!

MAN 4 *(overacting)*: I am not the Christ.

MAN 5 *(as a small man with high, querulous voice)*: There are rumors. They say you are Elijah.

MAN 4: Elijah? No!

MAN 2 *(as a suspicious one, peering around at the crowd)*: Are you a new prophet?

MAN 4: Nay! Not a prophet.

MAN 3 *(the pompous one again)*: Who are you then? Ah—Jerusalem demands an answer.

MAN 4: I am a voice crying abroad in this wilderness, "Make the way straight for the Lord." *He* comes after me! *He* whom I baptized. None of you—no! not one—is worthy to touch his shoe fastener! Make the way clear for the Lord!

MAN 5 *(again the old querulous one)*: Hold your insolent tongue! The elders will be told your words.

CHORUS *(variously, crowding him, to his pretended fright)*: Tell them. Go away. Leave us alone. We don't care!

MAN 2 *(the suspicious one)*: Let us return. These foolish peasants deserve their punishment!

MAN 3 *(the pompous one):* But they may bring trouble upon *us. (To crowd.)* Begone! What if the Roman governor hears? If the soldiers come, ah—some of you will die. *(To "John.")* You! You have influence with them. Save the lives of these misguided creatures! Bid them go home at once!

MAN 4: You hypocrites! You offspring of vipers! Who warned *you* to flee from the wrath to come? I baptized with water, but *he* shall baptize with the Holy Ghost!

MAN 2 *(the suspicious one):* He's mad! Let us go!

(Momentary pause, then all relax. The mimicry is done. Judas was caught up in it, reacting to play.)

MAN 1: That's—all?
WOMAN 1 *(excited):* All? Did you not hear us? Did not the Baptist say the *Messiah* was coming? Soon, he said. To their very faces he said it!

JUDAS *(eagerly):* He truly meant the Messiah? *(They ignore him.)*
MAN 5: They yearned to take him prisoner to Jerusalem. But he showed no fear.
WOMAN 2: But *they* feared! They dared not seize him with so many of us there.
MAN 1: They've gone
CHORUS *(variously as they leave):* Aye, they've gone. The little one was shaking. So was the proud one afraid. Aye! Did you see him stumble over his robe as they fled? Such haste! Such a *robe*—gold threads, did you see? Even the servants wore rich apparel. To think they came to see us. *(Exeunt, all talking.)*

JUDAS *(follows to exit, calling out):* Where may this Baptist be found? Where may I see him?

(Gives up. Returns to bundle, puts bread away and settles to sleep. All lights off except his.)

CHORUS *(off, in darkness, after pause. Garbled murmur, the normal speech, for the men. Women's voices sound high and far away):*

107

Look! There is the Promised One of God! *(Judas wakes, listens.)* Foretold of the prophets. He will take away the world's sin.

MEN *(off):* This is the man! *(Judas sits up.)*
This is the man I came to make known to the people!
This is the man I baptized!

(Women, off, simultaneously take sounds oo-oo-oo, o-o-o, and a-a-ah in continuous low sustained tones while the men continue in deeper voices.)

I saw the Spirit rest upon him. *(Judas stands.)*
I heard the voice of God!
I am his witness of these things.
I say to all of you—

CHORUS *(off): Here is the Son of God! (Brief silence.)*
JUDAS *(thinking aloud. Spot follows him. When he leaves his bundle, it is removed):* This Baptist—he is brave. The powerful, he fears not. A leader himself. Yet he acknowledges this *other* as greater. Is he then the Messiah? The Promised One of Israel? To such a one a man might fasten his hopes, even his life. I wonder. I wonder. To see the promised King come into his kingdom! To be one who served him! *(He has reached right, in thought.)*

CHORUS *(off):* Springtime of life.
Springtime of Messiah.
Beginning time!
(Man 1, as Andrew, comes quickly across back stage from left, calling to right, as stage lights come up.)

ANDREW: Simon! Simon, come quickly! We have found the Messiah!

(Man 2, as Simon Peter, comes quickly from right.)

SIMON: Where, Andrew?
JUDAS: Where is he?

ANDREW *(ignoring Judas):* This way. Hurry! *(Runs left. Simon follows, calling over his shoulder as he runs.)*

SIMON: Philip!
JUDAS *(urgently to Simon):* Where is he?

(Man 3, as Philip, comes from right, colliding with Judas and running on, in turn calling back.)

PHILIP: Nathanael! Come! *(Man 4, as Nathanael, also runs across, avoiding Judas. Exeunt.)*

JUDAS *(follows to exit, eagerly):* Where do you go?
FOUR MEN *(off, calling):* To Jesus of Nazareth! To Cana!
CHORUS *(off):* To a wedding in Cana-a-a. Come with us! Co-o-ome.

(Judas freezes as lights go off. His spot comes on center. Soon he enters the spot, bemused.)

JUDAS: It was *water*. This I know. I myself saw it drawn from the well. I tasted it —wine! Is he Messiah? Israel's King? *(Freezes DR.)*

(Judas spot off. Silhouette lights up as men gather center back. Two stools placed for Man 5, Caiaphas, and MAN 6, Annas. The others from either side of them. The Sanhedrin is in council.)

MAN 4: After our last report to this council, news came. A second prophet is in that desert country. *(Uneasy murmurs.)*

ANNAS: With followers?
MAN 4: Only a few. As yet. But if he is like that man John—
MAN 2 *(interrupting):* Be not troubled. Even now word has arrived— this new prophet departs into Samaria. *(Sounds of satisfaction.)* The Samaritans will deal with him.

CAIAPHAS: And the Baptist?
ANNAS: Yes, what of the Baptist?
MAN 2: His followers are deserting to the new prophet. Now with that one in Samaria—

MEN *(variously)*: A blessing. Jehovah be praised. Secure.

(Silhouette lights off. Stools away. Judas' spot up.)

JUDAS *(joyously)*: I must follow him! *(To stage back, closed position.)*

(WOMEN *join* MEN *stage back right and* MEN *left. Hereafter this will be called the set position. Stage lights up.)*

CHORUS: Summertime of life.
Summertime of Messiah.
Fulfillment time! *(Brief pause, change in tone.)*
Samaria! Hated and feared Samaria!

WOMAN 1 *(steps out of* CHORUS *and speaks to an invisible Jesus left)*: Sir! Give me this living water so I shall never thirst again!

VOICE: I am the living water. I am the Christ speaking to you.
WOMAN 1 *(urgently to Chorus)*: Come quickly to the well! There is a man there who told me all I ever did. Is this truly the Christ? *(Freeze in pose.)*

CHORUS *(after pause)*: Stay with us, Lord! Speak to us.
VOICE: For two days only will I stay.
CHORUS *(after pause, devoutly)*: We believe, Lord. We believe not because of what this wicked woman said, but because we have heard you ourselves. You are the Messiah. *(WOMAN 1 rejoins them.)*

JUDAS *(to audience)*: Even Samaritans! Surely the Promised One.
WOMAN *(chanting)*: He healed the leper.
JUDAS *(moving freely)*: I saw him!
MEN *(chanting)*: And the crowds followed him.
WOMEN: He healed the lame man on the Sabbath, And let his disciples pick grain to eat on the Sabbath.

JUDAS: I was there! I followed them!
MEN: And the crowds followed him.
WOMEN: And healed in the synagogue on the Sabbath, And defied the will and hypocrisy of the Pharisees everyday!

JUDAS: This he did. I was witness.
MEN *(loudly):* And the crowds followed him!
CHORUS: And the crowds followed him.

> Where he went the crowds followed him And *Judas* from *Kerioth* followed him!

JUDAS *(to left):* Master, may I come with you? Share your life? My heart is eager to serve you. I have the skills of a steward. A skillful steward is useful. *(He has moved left and freezes in pose.)*

CHORUS: And after a night of prayer, Jesus spoke to his followers, and named twelve to be apostles:

MAN 1: Simon, whom he called Peter,
WOMAN 1: And Andrew, his brother,
CHORUS: Fishermen.
MAN 2: James and John, sons of Zebedee,
CHORUS: Fishermen.
WOMAN 2: Bartholomew
CHORUS: Called Nathanael.
MAN 3: And Philip,
CHORUS: His friend.
WOMAN 3: Matthew,
CHORUS: A tax collector.
MAN 4: Thomas,
CHORUS: A twin.
WOMAN 4: James, the son of Alphaeus,
CHORUS: And Judas called Thaddaeus.
MAN 5: Simon, nicknamed the Patriot.
CHORUS: And *Judas* of *Kerioth.*
JUDAS: Simple men. It worries me. Simple men to build a kingdom? Can it be done? Still—if he can heal a leper—

(Woman steps out of CHORUS, gives a small pouch to JUDAS, steps back.)

MEN: Judas is our steward. Judas is skilled. He carries the purse for our company. *(CHORUS leaves right. Lights off except JUDAS' spot.)*

JUDAS *(looking at pouch with pride):* I will be faithful. *(Takes stool, sits left, still looking at pouch.)* Thin. Empty. When he is King, it will grow fat. Judas of Kerioth—someday treasurer of a kingdom? *(Fastens pouch at side. Freezes. Pause. Stage lights up. MAN 2 as Peter and MAN 3 as John enter.)*

PETER: Greetings, Judas! An opportune gift from that Capernaum centurion, even if he was a Roman.

JUDAS *(philosophically):* When the pouch is flat, a gift comes. We eat.
PETER: For the Master, that is enough.
JUDAS: Not for the treasurer. Peter, a store set aside brings ease of mind.
PETER: Why this concern?
JUDAS: For all these years I try to set some aside in the good times. Even so you were not stinted. But the lean times eat it up. Our store does not increase even with all my care. All my skill cannot take coins from the air, nor take the edge from your hunger. If the day comes when I cannot provide—

PETER: You worry too much about us all! You care for us like a mother.
JOHN: Peter jests, Judas. Through affection. Be not troubled. Our needs are simple.

JUDAS *(urgently):* When the Master comes into his kingdom, he can use such a store! John, why does he wait? Why not declare himself now?

JOHN *(shrugging):* He says—when his time comes.
JUDAS *(moving about restlessly):* His "time"? What is this "time," John? He talks of it often. What means the Master, Peter?

PETER: I know not. When he is ready, perhaps. During the while, he heals. He teaches.

JUDAS *(angrily):* He heals blind *beggars!* Lepers, demon-possessed *outcasts!*

PETER *(agreeing, as he sits):* Men.

JUDAS: *Poor* men! Like the sands of the Sea of Galilee.

PETER: He also teaches. The people. Us. His great words. His wisdom and power.

JUDAS: Verily no king could be greater! But the whole world must know. Confess—he is ready for his kingdom even now.

JOHN *(thoughtfully):* Then perhaps *we* are not ready.

JUDAS: No, no! Remember when he sent us forth by twos? We healed the sick with his power in us.

JOHN: Power *he* gave us.

JUDAS: This he could do again! We would be greatly useful to him. The multitudes follow him. Wherever he goes it is the same. Never will come a time more favorable. He must take his rightful place! Why does he continue to delay?

PETER *(rising):* Judas, Judas, I know not. Our love and admiration for the Master is as great as yours.

JUDAS *(bitterly):* But not so—impassioned? So—hysterical?

JOHN *(arm around Judas' shoulders):* Peter meant not that. Your love for our Master is deep and strong. Your devotion is to him. All know this. But, Judas my friend, a patient man you are not!

PETER: Without your devotion our entire company would lack. I meant only to remind you of those who oppose him. Now they are separate. Were he to declare himself, they would forget their differences. The scribes and Pharisees, the Sadducees and Herodians, the elders and the Romans—all would be joined together against him.

JUDAS: This need not be so! Have you not heard them cry for a sign from him? Many times! Only a *sign*. How easily granted! Why does he hold back?

JOHN: You see him with the eyes of love. Believe you that those who willfully blind themselves to him now, will *ever* see? No matter what sign he might give? *(He puts a sympathetic hand on Judas' shoulder as MAN 4, James, runs in from right.)*

113

JAMES *(calling as he runs):* John! John!

JOHN: James! What is wrong?

JAMES: The Baptist! The Baptist is dead! *(Shocked murmurs.)* Herod has killed the Baptist!

PETER *(shocked):* He dared?

JUDAS *(shaken, going aside):* It—it can't be true. He—who first said Jesus. Messiah?

JOHN *(as he, James and Peter go off right):* No error is possible?

JAMES: None. Already his disciples have laid him in a tomb.

PETER: The Master knows?

JAMES: He knows. His heart is heavy.

> *(They are gone. Lights off, except Judas'. Remove stool unseen. During previous scene, remainder of CHORUS scattered to places around the auditorium. They, with the audience, become a "great multitude." MEN 2,3,4 remain off right.)*

JUDAS *(after pause):* Dead. Dead.

VOICE: Let us go apart by ourselves and rest awhile.

WOMAN 1 *(in audience):* There! In the boat! Quickly! Let us circle the lake to the other shore!

JUDAS: I am fearful, Lord! Before it is too late, declare yourself!

MAN 1 *(in audience):* Speak to us, Rabbi!

WOMAN 2 *(in audience):* Heal my child, Master!

WOMAN 3 *(in audience):* My mother—only touch my mother, Lord, and she will be well!

MAN 5 *(in audience):* Help us!

OTHERS *(variously):* Teach us. Help us. Heal us. Touch us!

JUDAS: Let him alone! He has no time to waste. *(He begins moving about fighting against events.)*

VOICE: It grows late. The people are hungry. Feed them.

JUDAS: Out *here?* Even if there *were* coins?

VOICE: Feed them.

MAN 1 *(in audience):* There are but two small fish and five small buns. How far will such go among so many?

VOICE *(after pause):* Father, bless this food and sustain thy children.

WOMAN 4 *(in audience):* Look, look! There is food for everyone. Here, child, eat your fill. There is plenty.

JUDAS: If you will not send them away—*tell* the people, Lord! Let it begin *here! Now!*

VOICE: Gather up the remains. Waste nothing. The people will hunger again.

MAN 6 *(in audience):* Twelve baskets! Saw you the twelve baskets?

JUDAS *(in despair):* Their stomachs he fills, while a kingdom goes begging.

CHORUS *(in audience):* Master. Rabbi. Teacher. *(Then several.)* Be our king!

JUDAS: Listen, Lord! Listen to them!

VOICE: You seek me now because you had your fill. Not because you believe in my signs.

WOMAN 2 *(in audience):* We hungered, Lord. You fed us. This is a sign for us. If you are our king, will we be fed?

VOICE: Seek not food which endures not. Seek eternal food. Have faith in the One sent from God.

JUDAS: Proclaim yourself, Lord!

MAN 6 *(in audience):* By what sign shall we believe? Moses gave us bread from heaven.

VOICE: My Father gives you the true Bread from heaven.

MAN 5 *(in audience):* What is "true bread"?

WOMAN 3 *(in audience):* Give us this bread! We hunger again.

VOICE: No one who comes to me is refused. I am come down from heaven to do the will of the One who sent me. I am the Bread of Life.

MAN 1 *(to someone in audience):* What means this?

OTHERS *(variously, overlapping, to members of audience):* What said he? I cannot hear him. Are we not to be fed? I do not understand.

(CHORUS assembles stage right, ready.)

VOICE: My body is the bread I give. I give it that you might have eternal life. These things are spiritual, not of the body. *(Sadly.)* Some of you believe not.

JUDAS *(in despair):* They leave him! They are children! Truly they believe not. His words bewilder them. Frighten them. A king, a protector like a father—this is what they want!

VOICE *(slowly):* Will you leave me, too?
PETER *(off):* Lord, where will we go? Where will we find another Master? Your words promise eternal life. You are the Holy One from God. This we believe. *(Agreeing murmurs.)*

VOICE: Not all. I chose twelve. In the heart of one hides a devil.
JUDAS *(to himself):* There must be a way. Before they all forsake him.
CHORUS *(off):* Wintertime of life.
> Wintertime of Messiah.
> Shadowtime.

VOICE *(after pause):* Now we are alone. I would talk with you. The people—who say they I am?

MAN 1 *(off):* Some say John the Baptist come again.
MAN 6 *(off):* Perhaps Elijah.
JUDAS: Even now?
MAN 5 *(off):* Others say Jeremiah. Or one of the old prophets.
JUDAS: Open their eyes, Lord.
VOICE: But you—who are my own—who say you I am?
PETER *(off, lovingly):* O Master—the Christ! The living Son of God!
JUDAS *(with hope and joy):* They know! Hear, Master? Hear?
VOICE: Listen to my words. Soon I must go up to Jerusalem. To my death.
MAN 1 *(off):* No, Lord!
VOICE: Your hearts will know sorrow. For you witness my suffering. You see my humiliation at the hands of the council. You watch my death by Roman soldiers.

PETER *(over murmurs off):* No, Master! Not death!

JUDAS: This cannot be! Not the Messiah-King.

VOICE: Do not tempt me, Peter. There is no other way.

JOHN *(off): Why,* Lord?

VOICE: For this I came.

JUDAS *(crying out):* To be *King! Not* to *die!*

VOICE: Take heart. In three days you will see me again.

MEN: *(off, calmer):* What now, Master?

VOICE: Follow me. Deny yourselves. Be willing to give up your life for my sake. Then you will save it.

JUDAS: He can't die! We must not let him! I will not let him. *I* will not let him. *(Freezes. Pause.)*

(Lights come up. CHORUS, now a Passover crowd in a holiday mood, come from right, talking, excited.)

CHORUS *(variously, overlapping):* What said you?

  That the prophet from Nazareth came this way.

  I saw him yesterday.

  I've heard of him. Shall I now see him?

  What tales are told!

  My neighbor's mother-in-law he healed—or so she says.

MAN 1: I've heard him teach. Near Caesarea. His company of followers was with him. *(Sees Judas.)* Look! See that man? I've seen him with the Nazarene. At least I think so.

WOMAN 1: Well, is he one of them or not?

MAN 1: Perhaps there is only a likeness.

WOMAN 1: To make sure is simple. *(Approaches Judas.)* Are you one of the men who follow the Man from Galilee?

MAN 1 *(closer, looking Judas over):* Verily he is! *(To others.)* I saw this man with others trying to exorcise a demon. *(Grabs Judas by the arm.)* You failed!

JUDAS *(jerking away):* We failed. *(All laugh, which angers him.)* But the Master succeeded!

WOMAN 2 *(mocking):* With what magic?

MAN 5: Does his magic power come from Jehovah? Or Beelzebub? *(Laughter.)*

MAN 6 *(pulling Judas around):* Beelzebub, of course!

MAN 1: Did Beelzebub bid the Nazarene accuse righteous men of seeking his death in the Temple?

CHORUS *(had not heard of this event, shocked, variously):* Not in the Temple. Blasphemy. Traitor!

WOMAN 3: The council knows he is still in Jerusalem?

WOMAN 4: Perhaps they are ready to declare the Nazarene is the Christ. *(Laughter.)*

MAN 6: The Christ? A *carpenter?* From Nazareth in Galilee? No one will know from whence comes the true Christ!

WOMAN 1 *(pulling at Judas):* Where were *you* when the Pharisees sought to take your Master prisoner yesterday?

OTHERS *(variously, overlapping):* You told us not. Where was this? What happened?

WOMAN 1: I was there. I saw you not.

JUDAS *(trying to pull away):* Let me be! I was elsewhere.

MAN 5 *(they begin shoving him to each other):* Working your own magic tricks? Like master, like man!

JUDAS: Stop, you fools! He is the Promised One of Israel!

MAN 1: Blasphemer! *(They all scuffle, the women to one side shouting.)*

JUDAS *(he breaks free runs right, the shouting mob after him):* He is the Christ! You will see! You are fools!

(They are heard offstage, then sounds die and Judas returns from the left, in disarray and panting. MAN 3 as John follows.)

JOHN: Judas, come. The Master has been in danger!

JUDAS *(panting):* Not he only.

JOHN *(concerned):* Are you hurt? Who did this?

JUDAS: A *rabble!* The Master?

118

JOHN: He escaped harm. But we must find the others quickly. We follow him.

JUDAS *(alarmed):* Escaped? Escaped from whom?

JOHN: Fanatics in the Temple.

JUDAS: Why?

JOHN: He stood before them and declared himself the Light of the world.

JUDAS *(joyfully):* At last!

JOHN *(uncomprehending):* We feared for his life. But in the tumult he eluded those who would harm him.

JUDAS *(exulting, pacing):* We shall gather his followers—all of them.

JOHN: No, no! Only our own company.

JUDAS *(unheeding):* The ones who hear him teach, those he has healed. Hundreds there must be! We march on the Temple. They shall see. Those who denied him. They shall see!

JOHN *(unheeding):* Come. We must find the others.

JUDAS: Yes!

JOHN *(going left):* We depart for Bethany at once.

JUDAS: *Where?*

JOHN *(exits):* Bethany! When all is quiet, we will return.

(All lights off except Judas.)

JUDAS *(unbelieving):* To *Bethany!* (He walks slowly left front, freezes.)

(Chorus has gathered in set position. Stage lights up.)

CHORUS *(with spirit, calling out):* Hosannah! Hosanna-a-ah!
    Blessed is the kingdom,
    The kingdom that cometh!
    Hosannah to the kingdom
    Of our father, David.
    Hosannah! Hosanna-a-ah!
    To the Son of David.
    Blessed is he
    That cometh in the name
    Of—the—Lord!

Hosanna-a-ah! *(Softer. Judas comes, listens.)*
This is the prophet Jesus from Nazareth.
The blind and the lame came to him in the Temple.
He—heal-ed—them!

(The Chorus slowly dissolves into the Sanhedrin formation, the women going slowly off right. Judas follows, trying to talk to them individually.)

JUDAS: Listen to me! He not only is the prophet from Nazareth! He not only is a teacher, a healer! He is the Messiah! The promised King! It must be made known to the world. We must tell!

(The WOMEN are gone, the MEN in formation. Judas gives up, goes right front, thinking. Judas' spot off. Ready with red filter. Sanhedrin lights up.)

MAN 1: Annas, it is better that one man should die than that all of us should suffer. Is there no crime with which we of the council can charge the Nazarene? A capital crime?

MAN 2: You want our thorn removed by Rome?
MAN 6 *(as Annas):* For three years a thorn! Unrest follows him like a plague. With the Passover crowds—
MAN 5 *(as Caiaphas):* For our security, he *must* be silenced!
ANNAS: But skillfully, Caiaphas. No charge must come back on us. Pilate welcomes any excuse to lessen our powers.

MAN 3: Which means a legal cause. Romans love the sound of law. A trial and sentencing—all by law.

MAN 4: Passover crowds may hinder us.
CAIAPHAS: Or help. Can they be led to cry out against this false Christ?
MAN 4: But followers of the Nazarene are in the crowds also, Caiaphas.
MAN 1: Far outnumbered. Caiaphas is right. It takes little to turn a crowd into a mob.

MAN 2: If there is no control—

CAIAPHAS: There are ways and means to control while seeming to let go. Coins here and there. The right words. With the Roman passion for peace, our rabbit is roasted! Do you not agree, Annas?

ANNAS: One thing—we must snare our rabbit. If he is to be ready for the spit and the hungry mob.

(JUDAS' spot on, now red. He enters Sanhedrin area.)

JUDAS: Sirs, I would speak with you.

MAN 2 *(agitated)*: He is a follower of the Galilean prophet! I have seen him! *(He and another Man seize JUDAS.)*

JUDAS *(contemptuously unresisting)*: I come of my own will.

CAIAPHAS: Release him. *(Men resume places.)* Who are you?

JUDAS: Judas, son of Simon. From Kerioth.

CAIAPHAS: How did you pass our guards?

JUDAS: Your guards are fat and lazy, O Caiaphas.

CAIAPHAS: Now that you are here, what do you want?

JUDAS: It is more to say—*you* want Jesus of Nazareth.

MAN 3: He overheard! He is a danger to us!

JUDAS: The whole city knows.

CAIAPHAS *(cautiously)*: Suppose your words are true?

JUDAS: I can help you.

MAN 4: You? One of his followers? How can we trust such a man?

ANNAS *(to others)*: Not all who serve *us* are virtuous. *(To JUDAS.)* Why did you come to us?

JUDAS *(pretending injured virtue)*: I—I was *deceived!* I thought he was the Christ, the Promised King of Israel.

MAN 2: Why?

JUDAS *(as a simpleton)*: He—he *said* he was.

CAIAPHAS: You believed him?

JUDAS *(whining)*: Your worships, I am only a simple man. To deceive such a one as I is not difficult.

CAIAPHAS *(ironically)*: Now this simple man wants to cleanse his soul?

121

JUDAS *(whining)* I am an honest Jew. I freely confess my error.

ANNAS: In all your *honest simplicity,* you say now he is not the Christ?

JUDAS *(as a simpleton):* You blame me! But you know not how it was. He is persuasive. I believed.

ANNAS: But now you don't?

JUDAS: O Annas, he is only a man. A man who disrupts the peace of Israel and brings the wrath of Rome upon innocent people.

CAIAPHAS *(suspiciously):* Why not simply desert him? You are his "friend." We are his enemies. You want us to believe you wish to help us? Why? Because he deceived you? What is truth? Don't tell me it is to make amends for your transgression!

JUDAS *(pretended embarrassment):* Well not exactly.

CAIAPHAS: Ah! I understand. Now you speak true. For the first time I believe you. You want money.

JUDAS: Well—

CAIAPHAS: Well, why not? A man can't eat ideals. He must live. Even such a one as you!

ANNAS: The jackal eats the lion when he is brought down.

CAIAPHAS: What does our money buy?

JUDAS: A plan.

CAIAPHAS: Only a plan?

ANNAS: We can make our own plans!

JUDAS: But I, who know him so well, say that my plan promises success. Does yours?

(The Sanhedrin whisper together as JUDAS watches.)

ANNAS: No harm in hearing his plan. *(To JUDAS.)* Tell us.

CAIAPHAS *(when JUDAS hesitates):* The silver will be paid! The plan?

JUDAS: Take him quietly. Where few gather.

CAIAPHAS: How? Where?

JUDAS: With his closest disciples he eats the Passover meal. Afterward, his custom is to go to the Gethsemane Garden across the valley to pray. There is where he may be taken. In the darkness.

ANNAS: It sounds possible. How will our soldiers find him? How will they know him from anyone else in the darkness?

CAIAPHAS: I have it! You, Judas, will accompany the soldiers and point him out.

JUDAS: Why—yes. Then I shall see his moment of—*(Recovering quickly.)* I mean, I shall see that no mistake is made.

CAIAPHAS: Such zeal! You want that money indeed. Value for value.
JUDAS *(virtuously)*: As you say, your worship.
CAIAPHAS: Then let there be no mistake!
JUDAS *(elated at his deception)*: I will greet him with a kiss. This your soldiers will see.

CAIAPHAS *(repelled in spite of himself)*: A kiss?
JUDAS: The greeting of friend to friend. Let your soldiers await me near the Golden Gate. *(He turns to go.)*

ANNAS: Wait! *(To MAN 1.)* Pay him thirty pieces of silver.
JUDAS: That can wait.
MAN 1 *(tosses coins in pouch at JUDAS' feet)*: Take your blood money now!

(JUDAS slips pouch into cummerbund, freezes down left.)

ANNAS: May we never see him again.

(Sanhedrin lights off. Remove stools. Women join men for set position. Red spot on JUDAS. Stage lights up.)

VOICE: I would eat this last Passover with you.
PETER *(after pause)*: Master, my feet you will not wash!
VOICE: If I wash not your feet, my lot you may not share.
PETER *(passionately)*: Then wash all of me, Lord!
VOICE: You are clean. But not all of you. *(JUDAS looks around, moves center front, elated with foreknowing.)*

WOMEN: A betrayer!
VOICE: My hour is come. The hand of him who betrays me to my enemies is with me on this table. *(JUDAS examines his hands.)*

JOHN: Surely it is not I?
PETER: Nor I, Master?
JAMES: I, Rabbi?
VOICE: He knows. *(Disturbed murmurs from all.)* Go quickly! Do what you must!

(JUDAS turns back to audience, freezes. Stage lights off, red spot still on JUDAS. Fan now blows red streamers in front of spot giving effect of torches.)

CHORUS: And Judas, who betrayed him,
    Led a band of soldiers and a curious crowd
    To the Garden across the Kedron Valley,
    To the very place
    Where Jesus was praying.

(JUDAS turns, caught up in the magnitude of the moment.)

MAN 1: Master! Soldiers!

(JUDAS runs right, with excitement.)

VOICE: Whom seek you?
MAN 6 *(a soldier):* Jesus of Nazareth!
VOICE: I am he.
CHORUS: Immediately Judas went to Jesus, covered his face with kisses and said, "Hail, Rabbi!"

JUDAS *(to imaginary Jesus right):* Now declare yourself, Lord!
VOICE: Do what you came to do.
JUDAS *(urgently, frightened):* Declare who you are! Quickly, Lord, quickly!

(Women scream in fright. Sounds of blows, struggle in the darkness.)

MEN *(variously):* Seize him! Look out for his men! That's a knife! My ear! He's cut my ear! *(Crowd sounds just under next speeches.)*

JUDAS *(frantically):* This is the time, Lord!
VOICE: Stop! What mean you by this uproar? *(Softer.)* Let me touch that ear.

JUDAS *(bewildered):* What is happening, Lord?
MAN 6 *(soldier):* The blood—gone! Look, my ear is not lost!
VOICE: Put away the knife, Peter.
PETER: I will defend you, Master!
JUDAS *(pained, bewildered):* What is it?
VOICE: Think you, could I not call twelve legions of angels to defend me, only by asking my Father?

CHORUS *(clamoring variously):* Seize him before his talk bewilders us! Hold him! His men—seize his men! Pursue that one!

JUDAS *(running to left as if following the crowd):* No, no! You don't understand! He is to reveal himself. Tell them, Lord, who you are!

VOICE *(over sounds):* Why am I treated as a criminal trying to escape? Any day you would find me teaching in the Temple.

(Fan off. JUDAS down left, still in red spot. WOMEN to down right as witnesses. PETER offstage left. Sanhedrin in position. Stage lights up, dimmer if possible. Imaginary Jesus down center facing Sanhedrin.)

CHORUS: And so his trial.
JUDAS *(to himself):* No, no! Don't, Master.
ANNAS *(to imaginary Jesus):* Where are your disciples now?
CAIAPHAS: Where are the witnesses against this man?
WOMAN 1: He said he would destroy the Temple and build it back in three days!
WOMAN 2: He says he is the Christ!
JUDAS *(to self):* He is! He is!
PETER *(off, shouting):* I don't know the man! I am not a disciple! I

125

know not what you are saying! *(Unobtrusively joins Sanhedrin.)*

CAIAPHAS: Are you the Son of God?
JUDAS *(groaning):* He is.
CAIAPHAS: Why call more witnesses? His own lips condemn him!

(WOMEN begin soft chant: "Crucify him, crucify him," repeat several times. JUDAS grovels on floor.)

MEN *(variously):* Take him to Pilate. Condemned of course. Pilate must sentence him. That's the law—to Pilate.

JUDAS *(brokenly from floor):* Wait! This was not the way. Do you not understand? He was to declare himself. He waited and waited. He said not the words. I thought—to force him! Oh, God help me! *(Audibly weeps.)*

(Crucify chant stops. WOMEN leave right. Red spot on JUDAS off, change to blue and hold ready. JUDAS drags himself up and staggers to Sanhedrin, holding out pouch.)

JUDAS *(weeping):* Take back your silver! Let him go!
ANNAS *(coldly):* It is yours. Well earned.
JUDAS: I didn't mean—Let him go! He has done no evil. Only good. Let him go free!

ANNAS: Cast him out! *(Two Men seize JUDAS, who jerks free and throws himself at feet of Annas and Caiaphas.)*

JUDAS *(frantically):* He is innocent! Do you hear? He has done nothing against the law!

CAIAPHAS: Leave us! We need you no further.
ANNAS: Go! What's done is done.

(JUDAS is silent a moment, then hopelessly rises.)

JUDAS: Then—I have betrayed innocence—to death.

(WOMEN, off, begin chant, whispering, then softly: He has

betrayed innocent blood," *repeat several times.)*

CAIAPHAS: Be reasonable. Constantly he has threatened our peace with Rome.

JUDAS *(weeping):* Death he does not deserve. In all his life, never did he harm a single creature. You can't kill him!

ANNAS: True. Under the law we can't. But Pontius Pilate can. With our assistance, he will. The trouble ends with Jesus of Nazareth on a Roman cross. *(To MEN.)* Remove him.

(MEN and JUDAS struggle frantically, JUDAS shouting as he fights.)

JUDAS: Listen to me! He is the true Son of God! He is the looked for Messiah-King! Listen to me! *(One final push and JUDAS is at left front. Blue spot on JUDAS. All other lights off.)*

WOMEN *(off, cease chant and whisper loudly):* That is Judas the traitor!

JUDAS *(hopelessly):* I meant not that! I meant not that! Does none believe me?

WOMEN *(off):* Judas the traitor!

JUDAS *(breaking):* Did he not know why? What have I done? O God, forgive me! *(Weeping.)* Why did he not speak out? Why? Why?

(WOMEN again take up chant, overlapping his last speech, "He has betrayed innocent blood" repeat. Begins as loud whisper, becomes vocal. In darkness the MEN in the Sanhedrin join in the chant. Volume gradually rises through following action, reaches loud climax when JUDAS' spot goes off. All this during action following.)
(JUDAS stares at pouch for a time. Then violently throws it stage center. Covers face with hands for a time, rocking back and forth in anguish. All very slow. Looks up in torment. Then slowly, agonizingly, as in slow motion, unwinds his cummerbund. Looks at it in his hands for a long time. Then he slowly ties a noose in one end. Then, holding it in his hands out before him, almost like an offering, he slowly crosses, stiffly, already a

dead man, and off. When he is off, his spot off and chant ceases abruptly. MAN 2 slips off stage left as Sanhedrin lights come on. Somber mood.)

CAIAPHAS *(rises, picks up pouch):* What is to be done with this?

ANNAS *(rises, joins him):* It may not be used in the Temple. That is the law.

MAN 2 *(enters, all turn to him):* The traitor, Judas, is dead. He hanged himself. But poorly. The cloth gave way and he fell to rocks below.

ANNAS: It is just as well, poor wretch.

MAN 1: Betrayer and betrayed, both dead. That is double blood money.

CAIAPHAS: According to law, these coins still remain his property.

MAN 3: His body needs a burial place.

CAIAPHAS: True. Then let us buy a field, a burial place for such as he.

ANNAS: So be it. Let it be called Field of Blood.

(WOMEN join men in set position. Stage lights on full then if possible dim slowly to the end. This is slow. WOMEN pick up last word in each line in soft chant, which they continue under MEN'S next line. MEN do not stop.)

MEN: They took the thirty pieces of silver, *(WOMEN begin "silver.")*
The going price of a slave, *(Change to "slave.")*
The price of a prophet from Nazareth, *(Change to "Nazareth.")*
And they bought a Potter's Field, *(Change to "field.")*
In the name of Judas of Kerioth. *("Kerioth" three times and stop.)*

WOMEN *(in high, far-away voices):* Juda-a-as, son of Simo-o-onnn, stewa-a-ard. . . .
Juda-a-as, son of Simo-o-onnn, treasurer-r-r. . . .

CHORUS *(in loud, hissing whisper):* JUDASSSS! SSSon of SSSimon! TRAITOR-R-R-R!

(Lights off, actors off.)